True Haunting

Edwin F. Becker

authorHOUSE®

AuthorHouse™
1663 Liberty Drive
Bloomington, IN 47403
www.authorhouse.com
Phone: 1-800-839-8640

All names that have been *italicized* have been changed to shield
the identity and maintain the privacy of those involved.

First published by AuthorHouse 8/25/2011

ISBN: 978-1-4634-0860-2 (e)
ISBN: 978-1-4634-0861-9 (dj)
ISBN: 978-1-4634-0862-6 (sc)

Library of Congress Control Number: 2011908868

Printed in the United States of America

Any people depicted in stock imagery provided by Thinkstock are models,
and such images are being used for illustrative purposes only.
Certain stock imagery © Thinkstock.

This book is printed on acid-free paper.

This book is dedicated to the psychic, Joseph DeLouise, A kind and gifted man who came to our aid and tried his best to help us, when no one else would step forward.

"Today we have laws that govern real estate transactions and in many states, demand that evidence of a haunting must be disclosed prior to the sale of such property."

This was not the case in the year 1970.
Edwin F. Becker, 2011.

Introduction

This is a true ghost story. It was written to be educational, as well as entertaining. Some years ago, when evaluated by a major publisher--although they liked my manuscript and considered it for publication--it would be **only** if I could 'remember' a few additional "dramatic-type" occurrences. I refused, for my intent was to tell only the truth, with no enhancements. Not allowing editors to manipulate you, is a true benefit of self-publishing.

The year was 1970, and this was likely the first haunting ever televised and reported by the news. NBC's Carole Simpson was the local Chicago reporter at the time. Author Tom Valentine initially investigated it, and called in the nationally known psychic, Joseph DeLouise. Joseph collaborated with the late Reverend William Derl-Davis, an exorcist from England. Our story was written about in the National Tattler, a news tabloid—although, somewhat inaccurately. Various types of psychics and investigators tried their hand at communicating, or 'evicting' these spirits, all unsuccessfully. This was the first parcel of real estate we had ever purchased and we were young and naïve, with ghosts being the last thing on our minds, not to mention it being a taboo subject in 1970. There was no 911, and the word 'paranormal' was a nearly unknown term. No, I didn't rely on my memory of 40 years ago, as this was actually written nearly 30 years ago, intended for family.

There are good ghosts and there are bad ghosts, and this building was home to both. In the process of owning this building, I learned many things about ghosts that I will share with you. Few people want to believe in ghosts. Your friends will say that they do not believe, should you tell them your house is haunted. When you have a ghost, you learn quickly that you are on your own. Few will accept that you have a ghost, but believe me...no one wants to sleep over. Ghosts cannot be exorcised. This is a fact, because ghosts are not demons. I believe that is why most religions avoid the very idea of ghosts. They simply don't know what to do, as there is nothing in "The Good Book" about guiding earth-bound souls to the afterlife. We found this out the hard way. In our efforts to rid the building of these malevolent entities, we did learn one thing--and that is that there is no explanation or absolute solution to paranormal problems. Expert after expert tried their hand at putting these spirits to rest...all unsuccessfully.

Ghosts, for some unexplained reason, are trapped in our dimension. Maybe a death that was so sudden that the soul of the person never accepted the afterlife. Maybe they have no idea that they are truly dead. Maybe it was the method of their death that binds them here. It seems suicide is sometimes a common denominator in this phenomena. The fact that one may not want to live any longer is not necessarily synonymous with being prepared to die and accept the hereafter. Then again, maybe suicide dooms them to walk the earth. Murder is also a very common denominator. A person's life is taken suddenly and unexpectedly, and they have no chance to reconcile their fate and in fact, may be obsessed with completing their various earthly routines. Possession of their domain is common. A house is the most common object that spirits cling to. Maybe they had their best times there, or their worst. Nothing is stronger than their sense of domain. Ghosts can also attach themselves to objects. Consider the case of a woman we know that owns an antique bedroom set. She regularly sees the former owner in the dresser mirror. She loves her antique bedroom set, and so did the former owner. The face she sees is an old gray haired lady smiling back at her. It has just become an event she lives with.

There are no specific patterns to ghostly activity. Much of the activity they create is to mimic their former behavior. In doing these common actions, we--the living--are easily able to explain them away. It is for that very reason that many times we fail to take notice. We keep looking for signs that are unnatural to ghosts. We expect to see smoke, glowing figures or blood flowing from a sink. We don't expect "natural" actions. Ghosts talk, move things, brush up against you, cry, and sometimes can be seen beyond the blink of an eye. Believe me, I know.

Ridding our home of these ghosts was a futile effort. Logically, if ghosts were so easy to remove, the castles in Europe would be ghost free, which is certainly not the case. These castles have documented ghosts that go back hundreds of years. Ghosts will come and go as they please. How and why they do what they do is a total mystery. To a ghost, we are insignificant. Sometimes they go through their ghostly routines uninterrupted by our very presence. Other times, our presence is taken as an invasion of their privacy and their reactions to our act of trespassing can be unpredictable. To a ghost, we are merely an inconvenience or an aggravation. Good ghosts may ignore you altogether. Bad ghosts might try and frighten you, at the least, and harm you, at most. I believe both types can easily send messages of their presence, but I also believe that we, as individuals, each possess variant levels of the ability to "see" or "sense" them.

The messages can be subtle or forceful, depending on the entity. The subtleties are many. How many of us have sat in a closed room, only to feel a cool breeze where there is no draft or windows? Or have watched a candle flicker, as if something had passed us by? How many of us have felt someone brush against us, only to realize that no one was there? How many of us have glimpsed someone walk across the doorway, or have thought we saw a person out of the corner of our eye, that really wasn't there? How many of us have heard a knock at the door and no one was there? Or footsteps in the hall when no one else was home? Has your dog or cat ever stared out at "nothing" and barked or hissed? Maybe it is the faint scent of something recognizable, but not appropriate. It could be a musty odor or the scent of flowers; maybe wood burning, or even bread baking. It is only for an instant, but never-the-less, is there. How many of us have awakened to someone calling our name? No one is there, so it must have been a dream--at least, that's how we rationalize it. Did you ever feel as if you were being watched? Ghostly subtleties can be varied and numerous.

There can also be stronger evidence. It can begin slowly. Items seem to get "lost". Items may move or are not where you think you had put them.

Some may fall or move in plain view on a regular basis. Electrical items turn themselves on and off, or lights will flicker. Voices crying, arguing, or screaming might be heard. You may perceive that they are distant; from an unseen television, or neighbors, perhaps? Ghosts can also be seen. They might appear transparent or then again, as solid as you and I. They might walk or float. They might throw things, move furniture, or slam doors. They might terrorize your pets. Worst of all, they just may try to harm you. Yes, they can propel objects.

Ghosts rarely attack you by jumping out screaming, "Boo!" They measure your reactions to various events, feeding off of your emotions and building up their energy. They gradually wear you down. Once you have entered their domain, you are a victim, whether you know it or not. I was a true nonbeliever. I had a strong sense of personal domain. As far as I was concerned, even after recognizing the phenomena, my attitude was that it was them that should leave, for they didn't belong. Ignorance was such bliss. Initially, fear was not a factor, as I had no idea what I was up against. As you will read, my actions likely caused to further antagonize them. I even tried to have them perform for me. What I didn't understand, was that from their perspective, the house was theirs and it was I that was the intruder.

I hope this book serves to help and educate those readers that dare to absorb the lessons contained within these pages. First, you will learn that ghosts indeed exist. I will offer you many of the signs that they exhibit prior to forceful activity. Ghosts will gradually move into your life until they taste your fear and dominate your behavior. Understand that they can harm you if that is their intent. Should you be thinking of buying an old house, pay attention to the feeling. If a room seems abnormally or inconsistently cold, pay special attention. If the little hairs on your neck stand up, take note; there may be a good reason. Don't ignore the goose bumps. Take notice if the air seems heavy. Take the time to learn the history of the house; it may save you money, sanity, and just maybe…your life. But if you have made the same mistake that we did and accidentally bought a truly haunted house, take my advice; don't wait as long as we did, because nothing or no one can help you. So just cut your losses, and get out quick.

Edwin F. Becker

"Knockings are a common ghostly manifestation.
In many cases, footsteps will be heard as well."

Joseph DeLouise, Psychic, 1971.

Chapter One

A Naïve Purchase

It was July 25th, 1970, when I saw the real estate advertisement for a two-flat apartment building on the near-north side of Chicago. A "two-flat" is an apartment building with two separate residences. It was offered as an heir estate, which (to me) meant that they were liquidating the property and would be more flexible on the price and terms. It was also my 24th birthday and a Sunday, but I would skip any celebration and I would soon be on my way to appraise this property, for my wife and I were desperate to find a new place to call home.

The reason for my desperation was my wife, Marsha, was seven months pregnant, and we had been given an ultimatum to move by our landlady, the kindly Mrs. *Newaski*, who was a wonderful old woman that owned our apartment building. She was not so kind, however, when she coldly informed me that she didn't want kids in her apartments. This was a common attitude of landlords during this period of history. It was a time when landlords could dictate most anything and be within their rights. I will never forget driving to her home in a near suburb to pay the rent for the month of June. It was at that time that I happily announced the fact that I was about to become a new father. Instead of the expected congratulations, Mrs. *Newaski*, the dear old Polish lady, stared at me and flatly stated, "So you'll be moving out soon?" I understood perfectly what she meant. In her

1

own way, she was stating that no children were allowed. My drive home was not very pleasant.

Looking for a new apartment was difficult and near impossible. As I scanned the classified section week after week, the best apartments clearly advertised for no children. This was absolutely legal in its day. We had been married three years, but had saved very little money, so purchasing a house would be near impossible, as a conventional mortgage required a 20% down payment. I was earning a meager salary as a computer programmer in the second year of my career. Computers were new at that time, and few companies could afford one. So I was fortunate to even have a job in my chosen field. Automation was not the lucrative field that it would become in a just a few more years with the explosion of new technology.

Yes, these were the "old" days, when a fax machine was the latest ground-breaking office tool, and people were beginning to talk about a new device called "calculators". We still had typewriters, comptometers, and cash registers that had numbered levers as keys. Secretaries still had to know short hand, because there were no hand held tape recorders--only bulky dictating machines. We used lots of carbon paper for copies, and record keeping was mostly done manually in various handwritten methods.

"Heir estate" clearly meant that someone had died, and the building was being liquidated by their heirs. I would proceed to go and take a look on my own, as Marsha didn't feel well and was suffering from symptoms of her pregnancy. She was barely five feet tall and already was as big as beach ball, with two more months yet to go. She was also still working as a keypunch operator. Keypunching was an early form of data entry. She typed data-- little holes--into cards that were then fed to giant accounting machines, or to the original huge computers. This was long before video monitors, or "CRT's," became common in the workplace. Marsha was working 50 hours a week and was trying to continue right up to the last weeks of her pregnancy. She certainly was entitled to rest on this day. I had no qualms about making a commitment on my own, should the opportunity develop.

I called the real estate company and was told the building was having an open house and that I could proceed directly to the address. I kissed my wife goodbye and was off on my adventure. We lived on the far northwest side of Chicago, which meant that I had a 20 minute drive to the inner-city.

I was somewhat familiar with the area, for at one time in my childhood, my family lived a half mile from the Campbell Street address. I knew it was within a short distance of the Catholic Church.

This neighborhood was just southeast of Logan Square, which was (then) primarily a Polish area of the city. As I drove through Logan Square, it brought back the memories of the trips I had taken with my Grandmother, who would shop at the various ethnic stores on Milwaukee Avenue. These were some of my fondest early-childhood memories.

The drive also brought back other childhood memories not so pleasant. I had grown up in Chicago, primarily in the inner-city. My mother and father were separated for most of their marriage; thus, I was shuttled between the two of them, living here and there throughout the city. Yes, I knew exactly where I was going. My destination was once a German/Polish neighborhood, and was now changing over to a racial mixing pot. This didn't bother me, but I worried about how Marsha would accept it. Marsha had grown up in Tulsa, Oklahoma; a clean, spacious modern City--quite different from Chicago, and this big city frightened her. As I drove, I knew that if I could acquire this building for a very small down payment, I would make it viable, one way or another.

I viewed it as a mere stepping stone. We could live there for five or six years and then move up to a better neighborhood or a nicer suburb. My plan was that if we could rent out one apartment, it would help pay the mortgage and we could live a much easier life, financially. In five or six years we would develop equity, and possibly the building would appreciate in value. Then we could add to our savings and allow the property to take us to the next level. This was the optimism I was armed with as I drove. I was prepared for anything. If the building needed work, I could fix it up. As I drove past the old Church, I soon made the turn onto Campbell Street.

Just a short distance from the Church was the Campbell Street apartment building. It was just down from the corner. On the corner was a frame two story building with a store front. Years before, it was common for every neighborhood to have a corner store where you could get a gallon of milk, morning paper, and a loaf of bread, plus the kids could buy candy. Those years had clearly passed. Quick and convenient stores had put the little mom & pop shops out of business. This one was deserted and boarded up.

A few doors down was a three story apartment building. Expensive in its day, it was a large, well kept brown brick structure. Wedged between these two buildings was the Campbell Street two-flat. Even on this sunny July day, the building looked gloomy. I attributed that to its dirty gray color, combined with the fact that it sat in the shade of a huge Elm tree that was positioned between the sidewalk and the street. It was also dwarfed by the larger brick three story.

It was a dirty, plain, old building. The architecture resembled something simple; it was as if it had been designed by a child. A tall rectangular box; functional, but not fancy. Had I known the term in that day, I would have described it as "Amish" in design. It was straight up and down, a few windows on each floor, and certainly nothing to brag about. It sat on cinder blocks, with a seven-step walk up to the first floor porch, which was a small, 5x6 ft area. Sitting on the steps was the real estate agent. He appeared as though he had lost the lottery, and earned this dismal field duty. Red faced and overweight, he sat, sweating on the front steps. As I approached, he spotted his potential *victim,* and greeted me in a friendly manner. "Hi, I'm Art. How are you?" We shook hands. I had never tried to purchase any real estate, and at age 24, I was inexperienced and fumbling for words.

"Could I see--er, look at the building?" I was clearly uncomfortable.

He sensed my inexperience and took command. I believe I was just the victim he had been waiting for; young, naïve, and desperate. "Sure! Let's start on the second floor, because a member of the family still lives on the first floor. She's as crazy as a loon, so don't pay any attention to her," he stated in a matter-of-fact manner.

We entered the hallway, and to the right was the door that led to the first floor apartment. It was a short jog to the left, and I was led to an enclosed stairway that took us to the second floor. As we started up the stairs, the door on the first floor flew open. Out pounced a dirty old woman that looked as if she hadn't bathed or washed her clothes in months. Her hair was a filthy, matted gray. The only thing dirtier in sight was the tiny poodle she cradled against her shoulder, like a baby. She appeared the perfect image of an evil, old witch, with the poodle as her familiar. She immediately started screaming. "Sons-a Bitches, you sons-a-bitches! Get out! What are you doing here? Sons-a-bitches, get out!"

I watched, dumbfounded, as she glared at us, also noticing the tiny poodle nipping at her filthy hair, as if biting at fleas.

Art was quick to respond with disrespect and authority. "*Myra*, get your ass back in there and shut up. You hear me? Get back in your apartment right now!"

As she slammed the door, I could still hear her muttering. "Sons-a-bitches! You sons-a-bitches…"

"Don't pay any attention to her. If you buy this place, she'll be gone anyway." *Art* assured me. By his quick and deliberate reaction, it gave me the feeling that he had been through this routine with *Myra* more than a just few times. It also seemed by the tone of his voice that he was tiring of this familiar routine. I stayed quiet in a bit of shock, because I was brought up to never speak to a woman in that manner, much less an elder.

The staircase going to the second floor was steep, dimly lit, and looked ominous, for it appeared dead ended, but turned sharply to the right nearing the top, leading to a landing and the entrance to the second floor apartment. The entrance opened to the dining room. Once inside, I recognized what was a complete disaster. Still partially furnished, everything was torn apart as if having undergone some type of vandalism. There was debris strewn everywhere. The floor plan was as simple and straight forward as the design of the building. From front to back, there were three main rooms; a living room, dining room, and kitchen. Off to the side of each main room was a doorway leading to three tiny bedrooms. Right next to the entrance was a door that led to the closet. Additionally, there was a single bathroom off the dining room, and a small pantry off the kitchen.

All the plumbing fixtures were ancient. The bathtub was a free standing type, with clawed feet. Today it might be considered trendy, but in 1970 it was just plain old. The sinks in the bathroom and kitchen were porcelain and iron, and supported by legs. Today, they might be considered "chic", but in 1970 (again) just old fashioned. Other than a homemade cupboard that served as a counter and an all purpose cabinet, the kitchen was bare. There was not much to see. As I looked around, my optimism told me that it was nothing that paint, wallpaper, and carpeting couldn't solve. We exited to the enclosed back porch. As we walked out, I looked up to a trap door on the ceiling that led to the attic. I was assured there was nothing up there to see and of course, I believed.

We proceeded down the back stairs and out the back door to the outside basement entrance. We were met by a musty odor. I could tell by the concrete work that the basement was built sometime after the house. The house was originally set on cinder blocks, then the crawl space under the house was dug out and concrete poured to create the basement. It only had a 6 foot height, so being near 6'3", I hunched over a bit as we toured. I could smell the residue of coal. It was a familiar smell, as years ago many buildings were heated with coal, which was normally stored in the basement.

Besides a laundry tub sink, there were three rooms partitioned at the side. These were called sheds. They were made up of nothing more than boards nailed together as partitioned areas. One was padlocked, one was empty and clean, and the third was the one used for coal storage years ago, and was filled with soot. At the front of the basement was a finished room, containing a large pot belly stove stamped U.S. ARMY. The smell of burning wood filled the room. The odor was so strong that I opened the stove, checking for something smoldering. Examining it, I could see it hadn't been used for years. 'Curious...' I thought. I took notice of the fact that it was very cool in the basement, but this was not all that unusual. Unfortunately, I didn't pay much attention to my goose bumps. *Art* seemed nervous and didn't talk much, which was a change. He allowed me to wander around, freely inspecting everything. I did notice his nervous feet always moving, as if ready to leave. I had the distinct impression that I was keeping him from something. I never noticed his nervousness was only apparent when inside the building.

We climbed the inside stairway leading directly up and into the dining room of the first floor apartment. *Myra* greeted us in the same manner as before. "Sons-a-bitches!" she yelled. *Art* yelled right back at her, and it seemed he had hit his limit of tolerance.

"Shut the fuck up, will you?" As they yelled back and forth at each other, I quietly continued my tour. Actually, I found the exchange to be almost humorous, as I went about examining her apartment. With the exception of the location of the front entrance door, which entered into the living room, the apartments were very much the same. I only took the time to peek into every room. I noticed that one bedroom was noticeably cooler than the rest. Again, I got a bad case of goose bumps, but it was dark in the room and I didn't think the temperature difference was significant at the time. In fact, given this hot July afternoon and in this un-air conditioned building, the cool air seemed a treat, if not a benefit.

We exited the back door of the apartment to the enclosed porch, and then we headed across the back yard and into the garage. It was completely filled with junk. "Needs work, but it could be a decent building." *Art* was now trying his best to sell me. What *Art* didn't know, was that he didn't need to expend the effort, for I was already sold. All I cared about was whether I could buy the building with practically nothing for a down payment. I didn't see anything that hard work couldn't solve.

The standard down payment for a conventional mortgage at $16,500.00 was a minimum of 20% down payment; so the odds of coming up with $3300.00 were zero. I wondered if the owners would sell it to me on a private contract, but *Art* explained getting all the heirs to agree was a definite impossibility. For an instant, I thought I was out of luck. Then *Art* began talking about a government mortgage program.

Within minutes, we were talking about an FHA loan for 5% down on a purchase price of 16,500.00. $825 for a down payment sure sounded more like reality. The only drawback, according to *Art*, was that FHA took four months or more to approve loans. I saw that as my advantage, not a drawback. I needed more money to close, for I only had about $200 to my name, aside from the money reserved to pay the hospital and doctor bills for our expected child, as we also had no insurance. If I could put the $200 down, I would have four months to get the balance by closing time. *[FYI, I was earning $82 a week after taxes and deductions]* I explained my situation, and *Art* felt it was not a problem. He told me the building had been for sale for a while now, and everyone would be flexible in putting a deal together. Even for the time, the building was priced right, but the question of why it was for sale for such a long period of time never entered my naïve mind. We quickly left for his office.

Minutes later, the contract was written up and I wrote the check for $200. The only contingency I requested was that the nasty old witch, *Myra*, was to be gone and the building was to be vacant upon closing. *Art* told me he would call me within 24 hours if the offer was accepted. We shook hands and I headed home a happy man. I had just bought my first piece of real estate on my 24th birthday. I could go home and tell my wife that we didn't have to worry any longer, for we would now have our very own apartment building. My only problem was convincing her that this inner-city neighborhood was safe and not as threatening as it appeared on the surface.

Before you get your stuff in an uproar, remember this was 1970. A woman's signature was not only unnecessary; it was nearly worthless in any financial evaluation and rarely required. The average woman did not work, and did not even count as a financial factor towards any commitment that a bank would accept. These were much different times.

Upon arriving home, I went about the task of preparing Marsha to accept my decision. I warned her of the buildings neglected condition, but assured her that I would work night and day to make it livable. She was as excited as I was, and completely trusted my judgment, for it sounded like a very good deal (considering our circumstances.) In a few short months, she would not be working and our income was to take a huge drop. Including her overtime, Marsha was earning almost as much as I was. I figured out that our mortgage payment, with taxes and insurance, would be in the neighborhood of $160 a month; however, we could rent out the first floor apartment for at least $100 a month. This would be a great help. I could also get a second job doing contract programming to pick up some extra money. All told, Marsha could easily stay home and care for our expected arrival with no worry. There was only one obstacle--if the contract was accepted, I had to take Marsha to see the building. I knew Marsha might see it as it really was and not as it could be, or at least, what I imagined it could be.

Remember, this would be rehabilitated the hard way, as there was no Home Depot, and home improvement centers had not been dreamed up yet. There were no "Do It Yourself" kits. It meant going to plumbing stores and lumber yards. Flooring, tile, wallpaper, and hardware stores would soon have me as a new customer. I would truly become a jack of all trades and master of none!

I would face that hurdle when I came to it. The next day, *Art* called me at work to tell me the deal was, indeed, accepted. At that time, I asked him to get me keys so I could take my wife through the building for a viewing on the following weekend. He agreed.

Saturday came quickly. Both Marsha and I worked on Saturdays routinely, so it was late afternoon before we could pick up the keys at the real estate office. As we drove, I tried to prepare her for what she was about to see; but nothing I could say was adequate for what we would experience. On this visit, my optimism was at a much lower level, as I began to face reality. I drove there, avoiding the immediate neighborhood by driving the boulevard. It was lined with stately old brick buildings with a park-like median strip in the center. We were soon at the Campbell Street building. Marsha was quick to notice that our new purchase was definitely the ugliest building on the block, but I countered with the fact that a fresh coat of paint could easily change it.

Being late afternoon on this cloudy day made the dirty, neglected building appear even more ominous. I held my breath as I turned the key, entering the hallway. I was anticipating the dirty and crazy old woman coming out screaming at us. I prayed that it didn't happen, for this would surely scare Marsha to death. For whatever reason, *Myra* did not venture out and "greet" us. I was in luck. I explained to Marsha that we would live on the second floor, reason being we could rent the first floor out for more money and the size of the apartments was the same. She agreed. We walked up the stairs quietly (as to not antagonize *Myra*) and we both noticed the enclosed stairwell was dark and forbidding. This was a common characteristic of the whole building. It always seemed dark. The interior absorbed light like a sponge does liquid.

As I had described, the apartment was a complete disaster. Papers, clothes, boxes and worn and tattered furniture littered each room. We took inventory of what we needed. The list was a long one, but began with paint, wallpaper, carpeting, and new linoleum for the kitchen floor. Despite the fact that it was a hot and humid July day, the apartment seemed unusually cool, much too cool for this hot, steamy day. We both agreed that we certainly wouldn't need air conditioning. I showed her the enclosed back porch, the back yard and garage. Then we ventured into the basement. Again, I smelled the scent of burning wood. Marsha smelled it, too. I checked the pot belly stove and once again found nothing that could put off that odor. I had goose bumps, but I didn't mention it. Marsha was clearly uncomfortable. When I suggested this is where she could do the laundry, she refused immediately.

She said she didn't like this basement and never wanted to come down there again. I assumed it was because it was so dirty. I told her that after I clean it out and paint it a bright white, she would probably feel different.

As we drove back to our apartment, I felt my work was cut out for me. I had to prepare the building to be fit to live in. I felt a bit sorry for my wife; she had come from an upper middle class family and grew up in a world that was unfamiliar to me, though I knew it existed. I was born of working class people. I was used to dingy apartments, no air conditioning, one bathroom, and the sound of police sirens from time to time. The inner-city didn't scare me; in fact, it was familiar and comfortable. I was very much aware of our differences in upbringing and I attributed nearly all of my wife's initial complaints to that very reason. I was sorely mistaken.

As months passed, we saved our money. My mother loaned me $500 to pad my savings, so it appeared I had more than enough to meet the closing costs, should the FHA verify my savings account. We were still waiting for the final mortgage approval when our daughter was born in October, 1970. Christine Ann, our first child, was born at Skokie Valley hospital. I had no insurance and both doctor and hospital submitted bills that basically wiped me out financially. I paid them in full, but had little left for closing, with only a few months remaining to figure out how to get the money together.

Just for your reference, the delivery and a three day hospital stay at a top notch hospital was $750.00! The bill for complete prenatal care and delivery, by one of the Chicago's best obstetricians, was another $700.00! Yes, things have gone up!

It was only a week later when the final mortgage approval came through. The closing date was set for November 12th. That same day, the real estate person called me to ask if crazy old *Myra* could stay an additional 90 days after closing. Needing cash, I saw this as an opportunity. I told him it was possible only if they gave me $120 a month for the three months in advance. I wanted $360 delivered at time of closing. I also wanted permission to start working on the building immediately in order to prepare the apartment for occupation. It took no time for them to agree to the $360, but I would not be allowed to enter the building until after closing. It was this $360 that allowed me, in the end, to close the sale of the building.

I didn't understand why I could not clean and decorate the apartment, since it was vacant anyway. As I tried to explain to them, the worst case scenario was that the sale would fall through and they would get the apartment cleaned and decorated for free. But they would not budge on this issue. They didn't want me spending any time there until the sale was complete. It was only at a later time that I truly understood why. It was because I would have possibly encountered what the heirs and Real Estate Company already knew existed. The building had very active ghosts.

The weeks shot by, and in no time it was November 12th and the closing was at hand. It was on this day that I first learned of the level of hatred that was embedded in this twisted family tree. Marsha and I (and our attorney) showed up on time at Chicago Title and Trust co., the site of the closing. We were met by the real estate agent, *Art*, and an attorney for the real estate company. We were also introduced to our closing agent from Chicago Title and Trust. Then came the big surprise.

Although the total amount involved in the sale was only $16,500.00, all of the five heirs showed up and each with their own attorney. I sensed the tension immediately, and could feel the bad blood. There was one other lonely attorney, which I assumed represented crazy old *Myra*, who was (thankfully) not present. Eleven people sitting on their side of the table, with Marsha, our attorney, and I on the other. As far as I could judge, the closing was moving right along. In transferring the title, deeds, and creating a new mortgage, I was constantly fed document after document to sign. The final act was to split the money up by deducting the real estate commission and expenses, dividing the balance between the heirs. It was at that time that all hell broke loose.

Apparently the real estate company charged $2.43 for photography, used to advertise the house. At least two of the heirs felt that since they didn't approve it, they wouldn't pay. Realize we are talking less than $0.49 per heir. A very emotional argument ensued and continued for about ten minutes, as we sat back in amazement. Everyone was yelling "I hate you!" to everyone else, refusing to pay the bill. Finally, *Art*, the real estate agent, dug into his own pocket and offered to pay the $2.43, which they accepted without even a thank-you. Because of the level of hostile emotion, I realized that this family was suffering some very bad blood. It would be months before I actually found out exactly how bad.

Once the closing fiasco was over, the building was ours. I had just signed my life away for thirty years, or so I felt. I now had the balance of the month of November to prepare the second floor apartment for us to move in. The real fun was about to start.

* * * *

I was obsessed with making the apartment livable. Marsha would not be allowed to see it until we moved in on December 1st. I called on my brother to help me. My younger brother, *Butch*, was still in high school, but I could pick him up on weekends to assist me. *Butch* was big for his age. At six foot, 190 pounds, he could easily do most anything a man could do. When I requested his help, he was all too anxious to come to the aid of his big brother.

That evening, I went alone to Campbell Street to change the locks on the outer entrance door, the second floor apartment entrances, and the garage and the outside basement entrance. It was about 6 P.M., and very dark. As I removed the lock from the front door, *Myra* came out to greet me. She looked like a filthy old witch, and was dressed in the same clothes as with our last meeting. She was still carrying her filthy poodle, draped across her shoulder.

"What the hell are you doing? You don't belong here. We don't want you here...we don't!" She continued screaming.

I remembered how *Art* had handled our last encounter. It was not my nature to yell at an old woman, but I felt it was at least a proven method of shutting her up.

"Get back in there!" I yelled back. "I bought this building, and if you keep this shit up, you're out of here...right now. So do me a favor and go back in your apartment and mind your own business." I stared directly into her hostile blue eyes.

She started laughing. Her eyes twinkled and she laughed hysterically. "You don't own this building," she laughed. "You can never own this building!"

"*Myra*, listen to me. I own the building. I agreed that you can stay for 90 days, but only if you behave. If you don't, I'll evict you."

"You own the building? You think you own the building?" She continued repeating the phrase, chuckling as she retreated into her apartment. I could still hear her laughing after the door was closed.

I had no immediate sinister interpretation of what she had said. "We don't want you here." I assumed the 'we' was herself and her poodle. The rest of her jabber, I figured, was pure insanity talking. I went back to my business of changing locks. I felt a chill when I went up the stairs to change the lock on the second floor apartment. It was cold and dark, with no electricity turned on yet. I worked by the light of my flashlight. I felt very uncomfortable, but I rationalized it was the cold, dark hallway, and the likeliness that old *Myra* could pop up screaming at any time that made me feel this way. Ghosts were the last thing on my mind. I didn't believe in such things.

I had grown up in the city, and being blessed with street smarts, the only thing I ever worried about was real, live people. Bad things can happen to you in the big city. Never would those bad things be committed by ghosts. If you walked through the wrong neighborhood at the wrong hour, you could get hurt. If you didn't lock your home or your car, you could get robbed. If you borrowed money from the wrong people and didn't pay them back, you might get a leg broken. These crimes that I knew as truths, were not performed by ghosts. No, I didn't believe in ghosts, but even if I had, they wouldn't have scared me. I only feared the real threats that I had grown up with. People could hurt you; ghosts couldn't do squat...or so I thought.

In a few hours, I was finished with the locks. I politely knocked on *Myra's* door. When she answered by opening her door quietly, I handed off the new key to the outside door. I told her what it was, and she cupped it in her hand, silently. Before she closed the door, I noticed there were no lights on in her apartment, but I felt that maybe it was her habit to retire early.

As I walked to my car in the dark, a man walked up and introduced himself with his hand extended. "Hi, I'm *John*. You the new owner?" We shook hands and I told him, "Yes." He went on to say that he lived across the alley and saw me changing locks. He said that he owned a second hand store, and wondered if I would sell the portable cement mixer in the back yard. I had walked right passed it and never noticed it. I told him I would make him a deal. If he would show up on Saturday and take everything out of the apartment on the second floor, he could have it all and the cement mixer too. He happily agreed. I wanted no money, for in my estimation, except for the cement mixer, it was all junk and I needed it all removed so I could clean and paint. I drove home feeling a sense of accomplishment. I was a landlord, and my family had a place of their own.

* * * *

It was a sunny Saturday morning, and I picked my brother up early. On this day, we would begin to transform that ugly, filthy, second floor apartment into a home. I had already purchased the paint and wallpaper for three rooms. Our first task was to move all the leftover furniture and any dishes, utensils, clothes, and garbage out the back door and onto the enclosed back porch. Once there, *John* could move it into his truck and sell it or junk it--I didn't care which. *John* showed up precisely at 9 A.M., as he had promised. When *John* finished, the apartment was completely empty. *Butch* and I could now start painting. We would do all the painting, then wallpapering, and leave the floor covering until the next weekend. We were both prepared for two long and hard days of work.

Butch would start in the front bedroom, which was just off the living room. It was to be completely painted. I would begin on the ceiling in the front room, before starting to wallpaper the walls. *Butch* disappeared into the bedroom and was quickly into his task. I never told my brother that the building was an heir estate. I knew someone had died, which is why the building was sold. I assumed it was the person living on the second floor, because old *Myra* lived on the first floor and was all too alive. At this point, he wasn't aware of *Myra*, for I felt there was no reason to tell him, since I no longer considered her a problem. I assumed my threat of eviction would keep her very quiet.

Butch was working feverishly, but felt bothered. In the rear of the bedroom was a closet that had no door. *Butch* kept glancing back at the closet and felt (as he explained) that he was being "watched." He was painting at break neck speed, for he wanted out of that bedroom. He didn't know why, but he was bothered.

I watched from a ladder in the living room as he painted the front wall, being quite visible from the doorway. As I continued painting the ceiling, I noticed he kept turning and looking over his shoulder. He had a strange look of anticipation on his face. I climbed down the ladder and walked in the bedroom, wondering why he kept looking back. Without saying a word, I looked in the direction that *Butch* seemed concerned with. An empty closet is all I could see. I walked into the closet and examined the interior, and it was empty. As I looked down at the floor, I saw it...a very old Ouija board. It was leaning against the wall, and couldn't be seen through the door. I assumed my brother had seen it, and that it was the reason he was so bothered. Some people believe that spirits can communicate through these boards, and I figured young *Butch* must be one of those people, as (at this time) I was far from being a believer.

When I picked it up and inspected it, to my surprise, he never knew the Ouija board was even there. We both examined it closely. It was very old, and appeared very well used. I removed it from the apartment, tossing it onto the back porch. It meant nothing to me. I had seen Ouija boards before, and felt it a mere game. I would later learn that I was wrong. My brother was clearly afraid of something in that bedroom. He never told me until years later, exactly how afraid he really was. All that time I had thought he was the fastest painter on the planet!

Butch soon joined me in the living room, painting the woodwork and the ceiling. It was about the time *Butch* started to relax and feel comfortable, working side by side with his big brother, that the entry door in the dining room swung open. In walked dirty old *Myra*. She was looking directly at us, and was laughing hysterically. It took me a second to realize that *Butch* had never seen *Myra*. His face was white as a ghost as he stared at the filthy old witch carrying her dirty gray poodle. Her matted gray hair was sticking out in all directions. She stared at us and continued laughing hysterically. Then, suddenly, before our very eyes, her mood of emotion changed in an instant and she began crying uncontrollably. Without saying a word, I walked to her and turned her around, guiding her down the stairs and back to her apartment. All the while we were walking, *Myra* wept uncontrollably. My brother was completely speechless.

I explained that *Myra* was a crazy old woman who would be gone in a few months. By the expression on *Butch's* face, it was no great consolation. I knew *Butch* needed a break, and it was time for lunch. We walked a few blocks to a nearby hot dog stand and ate our fill. The walk back did us both good. When we returned, I decided to explore the basement. We entered through the rear outside door. Upon entering, I immediately noticed that the shed with the padlock was still locked shut. I was instantly excited, because whatever was in there was now mine. It was the feeling of anticipation of possibly finding a buried treasure. I quickly found tools, and we broke open the lock. I held my breath as we opened the door.

Inside the 6 X 8 foot shed there was barely room to move. On each wall was a table and shelving, filled with magazines, as well as the floor. All were girlie magazines of some type, going back to the thirties. There was a whole collection of very old nudist magazines, plus more modern books, such as Playboy. Hundreds and hundreds of assorted magazines was the treasure that was locked in this shed. On the walls were pin-ups of women in provocative poses. I also noticed shoe boxes tucked on the shelves. I lifted a few shoe boxes and laid them on the table. One by one, *Butch* and I opened them. What we found completely blew our minds.

Each box was filled with pictures and cartoons of women or girls that were in some type of position that portrayed skin. If it was a cartoon that showed a woman with her skirt blowing in the air, someone had carefully cut it out of the newspaper and stored it in the box. If it was a photograph that showed a woman in a short skirt, or tight sweater, it made it into the collection. Thousands of these cut-outs stored neatly in shoe boxes, going back decades. This was someone's pornographic hide-a-way. Although young, *Butch* knew as well as I that this room belonged to a "sick" individual. I tried to make light of it, and started cracking jokes. I was concerned with my poor brother's experience on his first day at my new apartment building. First, he feels uncomfortable and finds a Ouija board. Then, old witch *Myra* enters laughing and crying at the same time, and now this! The only thing this proved to me was that old *Myra* wasn't the only sick puppy in this bizarre family.

Ghosts had never entered my mind. Instead, I felt sympathy for this family that obviously had suffered, what appeared to me as, some hereditary mental illness. I was now becoming curious about this family. I was curious enough to begin asking questions, but I would not investigate as of yet, for I did not have time. We still had plenty of work to do before the sun set.

We continued examining the rest of the basement. I had found a jar containing a few bullets tucked on top of a ceiling beam. I also discovered an antique silver plate buried in a small pile of coal in the old coal storage shed. This building hadn't burned coal for at least a decade. With each find, I wondered what madness drove someone to hide these insignificant things in such strange, out of the way places.

I stared at the room in the front of the basement that contained the pot belly stove. As I walked toward it, I could, once again, smell burning wood. Something was strange about this room. In the midst of this unfinished, dismal basement, was this finished room? Paneled with a raised wood floor, the room contained a couch, chair, and stove. It made no sense. The other rooms--or sheds as I called them--were nothing more than crude partitions made up completely of plain, unfinished boards. Crude as they were, it was what you would expect in basement with cinder block walls and a dug out, handmade concrete floor. But this one room was livable, and logically, just didn't fit.

As I walked out of the room and shut the door, it suddenly hit me. I examined the hasp on the outer door, as it was very old. The door was equipped a long time ago to be padlocked tightly from the outside. Whoever stayed in this room...was locked in. I said nothing to my brother. Not about the smell of burning wood, nor the padlocked room. I found these things unusual, but not disturbing. Given what I had seen in the "porno" room, and my experience with *Myra*, it seemed either of these "kids" would have been worthy of being locked up. So which family member was locked away? The smell of burning wood didn't bother me, but I couldn't explain it. *Butch* and I returned to the second floor to continue painting and wallpapering.

By the end of the day, we were exhausted. The apartment was finally clean. One bedroom, the living room, and the dining rooms were completely painted. Plus, both living room and dining room were almost completely wallpapered. It was a very productive day and I realized that, with my brother's help, we would easily finish the apartment before December 1st. It was the first time in my life that I appreciated the advantage of having a big little brother.

Over the course of the next few week-ends, *Butch* and I worked dawn to dusk and beyond, turning the neglected dirty apartment into my new home. We put new linoleum on the kitchen floor. We decorated the walls with half paint, half wallpaper, giving it a very trendy look. The wall that housed the cupboard and gas stove was covered in a textured red fake brick. All in all, it was a far cry from what we encountered just a few short weeks before.

I tried as best I could to "lighten" the place up. Since the apartment's light fixtures were old and dim, with most accommodating only one light bulb, I shopped for new ones that would hold multiple bulbs. I added a six bulb chandelier in the dining room and a hanging swag light to the living room. But, trying as hard as I could, the light seemed inadequate for the apartment. I could not eliminate the dark, shadowy atmosphere.

I desperately wanted Marsha to be happy with it, as she would spend the majority of her days there. Remembering her comment about not wanting to ever go into the basement, I ran a gas line through the wall from the kitchen onto the enclosed back porch. There, I installed a new gas dryer. We already owned an apartment sized portable washer, therefore she could do the wash in the kitchen and dry the clothes on the back porch. Everything was ready to move in, for the apartment was finally done. Outside of our apartment, I still had hundreds of hours of work. The interior enclosed porch needed painting, the whole outside of the building needed painting, the garage needed cleaning out, the basement needed cleaning out and painting, and I had never even looked in the attic. There was no doubt that my free time would be limited for quite some time.

Myra would be out in less than 90 days, and *Butch* promised to help me in giving the first floor apartment a new face lift as well. I knew I had at least a few years work, based on the time I had available, but it was my building…so it wasn't just work; it was an investment.

We were ready to move in. December 1st was a weekday, so my brother wouldn't be available to help me move. I didn't ask him to skip school, and instead, I asked my best friend, *George,* to assist me. There was one problem…George was blind. He had returned from Viet Nam miraculously alive, after the soldier in front of him stepped on a land mine. *George* had been severely injured, losing an eye, with the remaining eye damaged beyond repair. It would be thousands of sutures later, combined with a strong will and a lot of rehabilitation, that he would survive and return home.

I intentionally asked him to help me because he was strong and capable, plus he needed the confidence of having purpose. His family was treating him as an invalid. They catered to his every need and even dressed him. I felt that being blind was not synonymous with being a vegetable. Whenever I visited him, it aggravated me that his family considered him such an invalid. I didn't view him any differently than I did when we were growing up... except that now he just couldn't see. I knew he would accept the challenge of helping me if I asked him, and also knew his family would be slightly outraged. I asked him anyway.

George was all too anxious to help. He, too, had just become a new father. We both shared the experience of having new daughters. We had gone through the anticipation and anxiety together. I asked him and his wife *Ann* to be Godparents to our daughter Christine, which they graciously accepted. *George* was a true friend. Other so-called friends of mine made me totally aware of the fact that I had moved into an "iffy" neighborhood. Most held aspirations of moving to the more fashionable suburbs, escaping the problems of the city. Since I had done the exact opposite, it was considered a very bad decision. Though blind, *George* knew Chicago like the back of his hand and knew exactly where my apartment building was, yet he only offered words of encouragement and optimism regarding my new purchase. These were words I needed to hear.

We had met in our early teens and shared much of the same childhood backgrounds. We each experienced a parent that drank a little too much. We had each suffered abuse in different ways. We had each been "street kids" early in our lives, allowed to run around the city unsupervised. We shared the same street savvy and perception. As far as real estate, we both agreed that it wasn't where you started--it was where you finished that counted. *George* knew that this was likely my first of many real estate purchases. He totally understood that this was my first step. *George* also knew I was concerned about my short term finances. He told me not to worry about the crib for my daughter, who was still sleeping in a bassinet, as her new Godfather would provide a new white canopy crib as a christening present. He agreed to being picked up early on moving day. This was despite the protests of his family, who felt that because of his blindness, he was incapable. He told me that if I could carry the front and lead him, he could certainly carry the back and follow. It seemed everything was going my way!

"There is a difference between a ghost and a spirit, though
both of them are surviving minds of dead persons.
A ghost often seems to reject that it is dead."
Joseph DeLouise, Psychic Mission, 1970.

Chapter Two

The Awakening

Moving day was exciting. My parents had owned a home for a brief period in my early years, but all in all, I had come from a family of apartment dwellers. This fact made the day more significant, for I was now a land baron and this was my apartment building. A landlord at age 24…it was a true feeling of accomplishment.

George, despite his blindness, was as helpful as anyone sighted. Together, we moved all our furniture and belongings. I took the front and led the way, while *George* carried the rear and held his own. It took all day to vacate our old first floor apartment, load the truck, and unload it to our new second floor home.

Crazy old *Myra*, kept to herself, only peeking out the first floor window from time to time, studying our every move. I could see her peering out, as if in disbelief of the fact that "strangers" were moving into what was once her family's building. Regardless of her outrageous behavior, I couldn't help but feel sorry for her. I realized I was to put up with her for 90 days, but after that, I wondered who would take her? Where was this poor, insane old woman to go? I hoped her family would get her some help.

It was raining all day long. This became almost a tradition with Marsha and me, as it seemed that every time we moved, it rained. Lugging stuff up and down stairs, *George* and I maintained our old sense of humor. I was not yet used to his blindness, and occasionally ran him into objects or forgot to tell him to step up or step down. Fortunately, all of the accidents I caused were minor. George's blindness did provide insight to our near future, because blind people possess a level of hearing that is far beyond those of the sighted community. They can also possess a "sixth" sense that is far more developed than that of sighted people. It was this fact that, I assumed, caused George to ask, "Who's there?" from time to time. It was my assumption that he was hearing sounds that I was unaware of. I would assure George that no one but the two of us were around, and never noticed that these questions were always confined to the Campbell Street building. We would be resting on the stairs of an empty hallway, and George would turn sharply, as if someone or something was behind him. My blind friend seemed to sense a presence, and all the while I assumed he was just hearing things.

As fast as George and I could bring things into our new apartment, Marsha would put them away. By the end of the day we were well settled into our new home. The bedroom at the front of the apartment, which was off the living room, became our new daughter's. The middle bedroom, which was off the dining room, became ours. The third bedroom, off the kitchen, became Christine's play room. Marsha's mother had come up from Oklahoma for the birth of our child, and had bought Christine the matching dresser to the new canopy crib that was a gift from George, her soon to be Godfather. Marsha and I bought wall decorations and a lamp that were colorful, to help make the baby's room bright and cheerful. It was the nicest and brightest room in the apartment.

The balance of the apartment was furnished in what I called "early Frankenstein." Although most of the furniture was fairly new, we had acquired each piece individually and randomly at various sales, so rarely did anything match. Marsha did the optimum to arrange things so that they appeared at their best, giving it her maximum effort in making the apartment "home."

At the end of the day, after driving him home, George's family was relieved when I delivered him not much worse for the wear. He survived a day of strenuous manual labor. I believe it was a turning point in his mental rehabilitation, and after this day, he was now allowed to put on his own socks. I could tell that he no longer felt the part of an invalid, and he started refusing to be treated in that manner. There was no way for me to thank him properly. I could only hope the future might provide me the opportunity.

I was exhausted and had to work the next day. My job required me to work 10 hours a day during the week and 5 hours on Saturday. It was my habit of being early to work, so to be there respectively before 7 A.M., I had to be up at 5 A.M. every morning. It was this first morning that I would experience my initial encounter with one of the ghosts that had decided to be playful.

Marsha was always an early riser and would awaken an hour before me, spending time reading in the wee hours of the morning. Marsha would wake me by gently stroking my hand or kissing my forehead. I would then hold out my hand and she would place a lit cigarette between my fingers. After about three puffs, I was ready to rise and meet the day. There was always a fresh cup of coffee awaiting me in the kitchen.

This apartment had no shower, so I was forced to take a bath in the mornings. As I walked to the kitchen for my coffee, I stopped at the bathroom and started my bath. I put the old rubber stopper in the drain and adjusted the two-handle faucet to just the right water temperature. I left the water running and continued into the kitchen, where Marsha and I enjoyed small talk until my coffee was finished. Then it was off to my bath. As I entered the bathroom, I shook my head in disbelief. The chain on the old rubber stopper was wrapped around the faucet and the tub was empty. The faucet was still running full blast, with all the water going down the drain. I could have sworn I put the stopper in the drain solidly, but obviously, I must have been mistaken.

I put the stopper in the drain and sat in the tub as it slowly filled with what was now warm water, since most of the hot water had been wasted. I truly assumed it was my mistake and thought nothing more of it. Within minutes I was off to work, leaving Marsha alone. At work, I spent most of the day talking about my new building. More than a few times I would call home to see how Marsha was doing. However, I wasn't able to get through because the phone line was "busy." I can still remember being aggravated by the fact that Marsha would be on the phone all day. Besides not being able to get through to her, I heard the cash register ringing on our phone bill, because even local calls were measured and charges were applied back then.

When I arrived home, I unloaded on my wife about the phone. First, I felt that it was inconsiderate, because she should have known I would call to check on things. Second, it was expensive to be on the phone all day and we simply couldn't afford it. Marsha could only deny using the phone, saying that it was "off the hook" for a good part of the day and she never noticed it. Our second evening in our new building was filled with tension. We argued about the phone all evening, as I wanted to know how it could possibly be off the hook for so long, and if so, how did it got off the hook? Marsha could only explain that the phone was in the living room and she spent most of the day in the kitchen at the other end of the apartment, so she never noticed it. You must understand that getting additional phone jacks required costly wiring, not to mention the telephones were expensive and were commonly leased from the phone company for a monthly charge.

After dinner, I would start what was to be a nightly routine for quite some time, which was working on fixing up the building. I first had to get rid of all the clutter and junk that filled the garage and basement. I went down to the basement and began cleaning it up. First, I addressed the clutter, which would take me a week to empty out. Then, I had to wash it down before painting. I usually finished work at 5 P.M. or so, and arrived home before 6 P.M. It would be 7 P.M. when I was ready to work in the basement, and would usually put in three hours before retiring to bed.

When I awoke the next morning, I tested the bath tub again. This time I took great care in putting the rubber stopper in the drain. I pressed it in as tight as I could and adjusted the water temperature before proceeding to the kitchen for my morning coffee. After finishing my coffee and waking up, I went for my bath. Once again, the tub was empty with the chain wrapped around the faucet, with the plug dangling. This was a mere curiosity to me, but not frightening; nor was it shocking. I felt there must be a logical explanation for this, and I was going to figure it out. I would not mention this to anyone in the near future, and would leave it as my own private, mysterious, little puzzle.

Marsha found herself spending the day in the kitchen with Christine, who was content to be in a bassinet close by, or in her bedroom crib. This kitchen became the safe haven of the apartment. Marsha would make the kitchen her home during the day, and we would eat dinner or sit and talk in the evening there before I would continue my regular chores of rehabilitating the building. Neither of us noticed this curious habit until a much later time. Rarely did we spend time in the living room or dining room, because, for some unexplained reason, we were most always in the kitchen.

Marsha had her own little secrets. While I was at work, she would care for the baby by putting her in the bassinet and wheeling her into the kitchen. She would then do her laundry and prepare meals while watching television on a little black and white portable. It wasn't a few days before specific items in the kitchen began moving. She would awake to find dishes out of place or her broom or small appliances moved about. Being sensitive to these things, she was sure this apartment was haunted within the first week of moving in. Again, she would keep it to herself for a time, not wanting to approach this subject with her all too "logical" husband, as she knew what my reaction might be.

I noticed a change in our relationship, as it became tense. Marsha started immediately pestering me about wanting to return to work. We had agreed that she would not work until Christine was old enough to communicate, and I felt very strongly about that. I wanted our daughter to be able to tell us if anything was wrong with her care or if she was being abused. I couldn't fathom leaving our infant daughter with a stranger. In our first week, we fell into an almost constant argument about a number of issues. I was confused at the change in our relationship, but attributed it to the fact that we had just become new parents. Marsha and I enjoyed over three years of living with little or no responsibilities. Now we were parents, and within weeks of such, took on a thirty year mortgage. In my estimation, this was a logical cause for tension.

The reality was that Marsha wanted out of the apartment. She felt that returning to work was *safer* than staying home. She did not want to address the issue of a haunting with her skeptic husband, but she desperately wanted to escape spending her days alone in the apartment. I sensed her negative feelings, but I was certain that it was because this old building was simply not up to her standards. After all, she had never even lived in an apartment

25

until she married me; now we finally bought our own home...and again... it's an old apartment.

I ignored the tension and prepared for Christine's christening, which would take place just five days before Christmas. I called the Church and arranged the whole event. It would take place at 1 P.M., immediately after the 12 P.M. mass. The parish priest also agreed to visit our building and bless the apartment. We invited *George* and *Ann*, as they were to be the Godparents, my mother and brother, plus a few other close friends. As the days flew by, Marsha and I continued arguing about the phone. Nine times out of ten when I called home from work, the line was busy. Marsha continued to use the excuse that it was off the hook. In my estimation, the excuse was wearing a bit thin. I figured in about three weeks the phone bill would arrive and that would end the argument.

* * * *

Sunday, December 20th, was a delightful day, for it was sunny and warm for a December in Chicago, being about 40 degrees. We had bought the most beautiful christening outfit money could buy. Everyone gathered at our apartment for a short walk to the church. Our parish priest would perform the ceremony. This was to be a very happy day. The priest had agreed to join us for lunch after the baptismal ceremony and house blessing was completed.

The baptismal ceremony was short and simple. Watching my friend *George* offer my first child for baptism into the Catholic faith brought a tear to my eye. Afterward, we took pictures of Christine and her new Godparents. The priest wanted to change from his robes into his normal street attire before taking the walk to our apartment building. Marsha and our guests left immediately in order to get a head start in setting out the buffet lunch, while *George* and I waited for the priest.

When the priest was ready, the three of us walked together the short block to the building. I guessed him to be about thirty-five. He had brown hair with no trace of gray, with warm, brown eyes. He was your typical parish priest, keeping in close touch with his flock. I could tell he liked people and enjoyed this personal contact. As we walked up the front stairs, I could see *Myra* peeking out. As I turned the door knob to the entry hall,

I was shocked to find the door locked tight. I found this strange, because Marsha wouldn't have locked the door, knowing we were following close behind. Before I could get out my keys, the door to the first floor apartment opened suddenly, and *Myra* was in the hall screaming profanities.

"You fucking bastard, go away. You son-of-a-bitch! Get the hell out of here! You fucking..." She was yelling through the glass of the outer locked door.

I unlocked the door and yelled right back at her, though I was in complete shock and totally embarrassed. We had hardly heard a word from *Myra* in weeks and now this. I needed to shut her up quickly.

"What the hell is wrong with you? Get back in there and mind your own business or you are out of here. I mean it! You had better shut up and mind your own business. If you ever do anything like this again...I swear *Myra*, I'll immediately evict you." *Myra* glared at the priest as she returned to her apartment. With her eyes still fixed on the priest, she continued yelling obscenities as she closed and locked her door.

"Go away, you fucker, you don't belong here!" She screamed her last words. I felt this was aimed at me, but would later find that her wrath was more likely directed toward the priest. I should have recognized it immediately. It was as if the parish priest represented some sort of a threat.

I was embarrassed and could only apologize for her actions. There is no way to describe the humiliation. "I'm so sorry Father. She isn't well, and she's a little crazy." Although clearly affected, he assured me it was okay and not to worry. As we walked up the stairs, I could see my brother's startled face at the top, and knew he had witnessed the incident. Meanwhile, *George* is asking "What the hell was that about? Who was that?"

We asked the priest to bless the house before setting down to our lunch, and he agreed. He removed what appeared to be a brass holy water dispenser from his pocket, and also a small leather bound book, from which he would read the traditional house blessing. He would attempt to proceed blessing the house, room by room. He began in the living room. As he recited the blessing in Latin, he shook the dispenser in the air to produce the few drops of holy water that would sprinkle and bless the living room.

As he raised it into the air, it literally exploded. It didn't simply break...the brass dispenser shattered into many tiny pieces.

The priest was now obviously bothered. He bent down, picking up the splintered pieces from the carpet. Everyone had a puzzled expression. Although all witnessed the event, they did not know how to interpret it. When he finished picking up the pieces of the broken dispenser, he arose and stated, "I must leave now."

I clearly saw the frightened, confused look in his eyes, but I didn't understand why. It was all too obvious that his voice was wavering and he was shaking. As he turned to leave, I was immediately upset and literally grabbed his arm. I was well-familiar with a house blessing, and what he just did wouldn't qualify for even an abbreviated version.

"Father, at least bless my daughter's room..." I pleaded.

"No, the house blessing was sufficient..." came the reply as he, again, turned to leave.

"No, I want you to bless my daughter's room!" I demanded.

"Okay...then, I really must leave." he responded.

He walked to the bedroom only a few feet away and said something in Latin from memory, not using his book. He was reciting in hyper speed. As he did, *George*, who could only hear, whispered to me, "Ed, what the hell is happening? Why is he leaving?" I could only respond that I had no idea. Although the good Father wasn't a new priest, I assumed that maybe he messed this ceremony up and was embarrassed. The whole event was confusing, leaving just about everyone dumbfounded.

George was holding an envelope that contained a donation appropriate for the priest's service. He asked me, "When should I give him the envelope?"

I replied. "Wait until he leaves; I'll tell you when."

As *George* was asking me "Why isn't he staying for lunch?" Before I could answer, the priest breezed by. He did it very quickly, turning briefly to say goodbye while he was still moving. The exit door and the closet door stood side by side, and as he turned and said goodbye, he opened the closet door and walked completely inside, almost closing the closet door behind him. Turning from his goodbye into a rack of coats, he quickly realized his error and came out just as fast, exiting the apartment door. His face was pale and eyes concerned. Our interpretation was that he was completely embarrassed. Everyone stood staring in amazement.

George was left standing alone with his hand extended, holding the envelope containing the traditional donation. I quickly grabbed the envelope and chased the priest down the stairs. "Father...Father...I have a small donation!" I called.

He paused on the front stairs and reached backward, extending his arm to accept the envelope. I had the feeling I was in a relay race and was passing off the baton. He said, "Thank you," as he continued his foot race back to the church.

"What the hell happened?" is all I could say as I walked back into the apartment.

"Why didn't he stay for lunch?"

"Why didn't he finish the blessing?"

"Did you see him walk into the closet?"

"Why did he run out?"

Everyone was perplexed and all we could do was ask question after question, with no solid answer. *George* and I were once professional musicians, so we deducted that when the priest's holy water dispenser broke, he had a bad case of stage fright and left. It was the only answer we could come up with. No one even imagined that the priest had been driven out by a fear of ghosts. It wasn't until some later time, that I was to understand that priests are not prepared to deal with any form of the supernatural, and he likely had felt the presence.

We all focused on his "stage fright," especially the fact that he walked into the closet and closed himself in. I felt the unfriendly greeting by crazy old *Myra* may have destroyed the priest's composure and he never recovered. In the end, we found humor in the whole situation. I was intimately familiar with the traditional house blessing. Every room of the house or apartment was to be blessed. Our priest clearly didn't complete the job, so I would call him at a later date to finish. I figured he would be more receptive to returning without the audience, given his bad case of "stage fright."

The balance of our christening party went very well, although the incident with the priest dominated the conversations for the rest of the day. This event became most memorable, for it would signal the beginning of a new level of ghostly activity. In retrospect, the attempted house blessing may have started an all-out war for possession of this domain. The ghosts would soon accelerate their activity.

* * * *

It was the very next day that Marsha would get a clear sign of a ghostly presence. Alone in her kitchen oasis, she was watching the small portable television. Christine was asleep in the adjacent play room. Hanging on a hook along the kitchen wall was a hand mixer. The same hand mixer that had a habit of "falling" on the floor from time to time. Marsha heard a noise; she turned toward the wall that housed the appliances, and watched as her hand mixer began to vibrate. As Marsha watched in shock, the mixer lifted off the hook. It didn't fall down...it lifted up a foot higher than the hook it was hanging on and stood suspended in midair for an instant. As she sat paralyzed, the mixer floated about eight feet in her direction and tumbled at her feet. Marsha could only stare at the mixer on the floor. Strangely, she recalls she was more amazed than she was fearful. Years later, she would confide that she had felt it was merely a sign that "they" were there, and were sending her a message. Although somewhat frightening, Marsha felt this particular incident was not meant to be threatening--only a signal of recognition. For some unexplained reason, the floating mixer would repeat its routine over and over during the months to come. Sometimes when Marsha was there, and sometimes when she wasn't...as evidenced by finding it on the floor in the same place...each and every time.

Marsha became quite used to the kitchen phenomena. The door on her dish cabinet opened on its own. She complained to me about it. Taking my leveling tool, I found that there was no way the door could swing open, because the cabinet was not level and it tilted to the opposite direction. When it swung open, it actually defied gravity. I messed with the latch a little bit and felt that it locked correctly, so I had no explanation other than some kind of vibration was to blame. What else could it be? I still had no clue and was searching for logic.

The kitchen light became the next problem. Marsha swore it flicked on a regular basis. It was a brand new light and I had installed it myself. It was not exactly rocket science, as it was only an old two-wire connection.

Everything in the kitchen was on the same circuit, yet only the kitchen light in the center of the ceiling would flicker off and on. I took it apart and pieced it back together with the same result. Marsha continued complaining and I had no solution or explanation.

I was not made truly aware of the full extent of these incidents until a much later date. Marsha felt that my logical and skeptical attitude would not be receptive to this type of subject. I was a creature of logic, and ghosts did not fit into my thinking. I continued my chore of cleaning up the basement. It was in the basement that I would get the first warnings that our natural human instincts provide. My problem was my failure to recognize them. There was always a feeling that I was being watched. I felt it immediately, but wrote it off to the fact that I was paranoid of old crazy *Myra* possibly popping out and screaming profanities.

I would be in the dimly lit basement alone and in the midst of sweeping or washing when the hairs on the back of my neck would stand up and I would turn completely around, as if to face the person I knew was there. No one ever was. Goose bumps would set in. Sometimes my body temperature would rise and I would feel agitated for no logical reason. Frequently, I found myself responding to sounds and anticipating someone's presence. When I would find that no one was there, I would assume the old building was settling, or maybe it was a mouse. From time to time, I would get a whiff of burning wood, causing me to check the pot belly stove, but it was never used. The sum of these feelings began to create confusion…but quite honestly, I thought I was working too hard and not getting enough sleep. All too regularly, I would hear a man and a woman arguing. From the basement, it sounded somewhat close and I assumed it was coming from one of the adjacent buildings. I never realized it was the same argument being played over and over.

I would learn that the shed that held the magazine and pornographic collection belonged to a son named *Ben*. I would later learn that it was *Ben* that died in the bathroom of our apartment, and whose death would cause the sale of the building. For now, all I knew was that this room with boxes of girly pictures carefully cut from papers and piles of magazines, belonged to *Ben*. Everything had his name on it. Eventually, while working alone in the basement, I began talking to *Ben* as if he were there with me. I didn't know why I was talking to him, as I did not submit to believing in ghosts... yet. I can only surmise that I felt it better than talking to myself.

Fortunately, I was born with a great inner voice. It is a voice that served me well growing up in the inner-city, yet confronted by something I could not see, I ignored every single signal my mind and body was sending me. Yet, my subconscious was taking some control, as I began communicating without even recognizing it.

I would say things such as *"Ben,* you old pervert, why didn't you clean this place up?" or, *"Ben,* what the hell am I going to do with all these magazines?" *"Ben,* this basement is a wreck, you lazy, old, perverted bastard."

It became a normal habit that I was complaining regularly to *Ben.* When I would find something unusual, I would ask *Ben,* "What the hell is this?" Or, if I was tossing it out, I'd mutter "Say goodbye to this, *Ben,* you old deviate." Whenever I was alone, I would complain to *Ben* or ask him questions.

The shed filled with the magazines had to go. I called around and found a local antique dealer who wanted the magazines, sight unseen, for sixty dollars. I said, "Sold!" All I wanted was for him to clean them out as soon as possible. Everything in the basement would go...except that old pot belly stove. I wasn't fond of it, but it presented a puzzle that I needed to figure out. Why the smell of burning wood? I figured old *Myra* had something to do with it. Maybe she was burning things when I wasn't around. So I set a trap. I selected a few pieces of newspaper, carefully tearing the corners off that bore the date, and I stuffed them in the old pot bellied stove. If she burned anything, she would also burn the papers and I would know it.

* * * *

I was proud to have Christmas at our apartment. My mother and brother came over for Christmas Eve, bringing along my favorite Aunt. Aunt Helen was suffering from breast cancer for years, and this would be her last Christmas. Aunt Helen would be the first person in our family-- outside of Marsha and me--to realize we lived in a haunted building. Our Christmas was pleasant and Aunt Helen didn't say a thing about what she felt. Her warning would not be until months later when she was near death. When she did give us her warning, I had flash backs of her behavior that Christmas Eve and her curious questions that didn't register with me at the time.

Aunt Helen spent a lot of her time in our apartment going from room to room. Sometimes she would stand in the doorway of a room and just stare. I assumed that she was admiring the work we had done making the apartment livable. Today, I now know she was likely seeing things. Maybe it was because she was "sensitive," or maybe it was the fact that she was fighting off death that gave her the ability to have a special sensitivity. I would later learn she absolutely knew we had ghosts.

Aunt Helen was curious as to how I found this building and what I knew about the family that owned it. At the time I didn't know much, which was a fact that she probably already knew. Today, I believe it was her way of telling me to find out what I was dealing with. Although Aunt Helen was known for her smiles and good sense of humor, she spent the evening in a serious mood for a Christmas Eve. Regardless of the pain, she kept her smile until the day she faced death; so in retrospect, her serious and apprehensive mood was obvious and significant.

The holiday weeks of 1970 passed without a problem. It may have been that we were too wrapped up emotionally in the season. It was our daughter's first Christmas, plus we spent an enormous amount of time shopping and visiting, being away from home. After the holidays, our problems continued. The phone was constantly off the hook. When I finally received the phone bill, I was surprised that Marsha had been correct. The phone bill was small, with hardly any calls being made. I was totally confused. If Marsha was correct, then how does the phone come off the hook?

In my estimation, I felt that something was going on, but I didn't know exactly what. I knew Marsha needed some company. This was the first time that she was confined to the house in her whole life and I thought maybe that was the problem. I decided to get her a dog. We already owned a cat, so I needed a dog that would tolerate cats. I also wanted a dog that was intimidating. Holly was the solution. She was a three year old shepherd and husky mix. Holly was wolf-like in appearance, with a strong bark; yet gentle as a lamb and Marsha loved her.

It was now January of 1971 when *George* started complaining that the phone was always busy. "How the hell can you stay on the phone all night?"

he would ask. It was in that month that I noticed the problem myself. I would come home from work and check the phone. In most cases, it was on the hook and appeared normal. After changing clothes and eating dinner, I would check it before starting my chores. Lo and behold, I started to find it off the hook and lying on its side. I was now aware of it and had no explanation. Rather than talk about it and acknowledge the problem, I chose to ignore the whole issue and treat it as a mere inconvenience. Marsha and I just began checking the phone at regular intervals, as if it was a normal daily function. We accepted it as part of our daily routine. It may sound ridiculous, but that's exactly how it was. There was absolutely no talk of ghosts.

Holly quickly became a family member and turned into a great watch dog. Now and then she would bark, as if someone was in the yard or on the porch, but no one was ever there. I assumed she was hearing people on the street or from a few buildings down the block. One night, Holly had good reason to bark. There were footsteps on the back porch. I could clearly hear them. They were slow, heavy, deliberate footsteps, sounding rather close. It was my assumption that it was crazy old *Myra*, since the outer door was locked to outsiders. As Holly and I went out on the back porch in anticipation of finding *Myra*, we found nothing. Going down the stairs to the first floor, we, once again, found nothing...not even a light on. These "steps" became a regular occurrence. Holly soon made it her habit to sleep next to our bed.

My daily routine was the same. Up at 5 A.M., be at work by 7 A.M., home by 6 P.M., work on the house till 10 P.M.--except on Sunday, when we would typically go shopping or visiting. Little things started creeping up on us. The door that separated the kitchen from the rest of the apartment wouldn't stay closed. In the evening, when the baby was put to sleep, Marsha would stay in the kitchen and close the door, so as to not disturb the baby. The door was an old, painted-over oak door that closed tight--in fact, it often stuck and was hard to open, due to all the layers of paint. We could never figure out why it would open on its own? Again, we accepted it and it became routine to just close it...and close it...and close it.

Then the arguing that I was already so familiar with started to be heard later at night. It was usually after we went to bed. It sounded like a man and woman yelling at each other. The first time we heard it from inside the apartment, it sounded as if it was on our back porch. Since we knew that couldn't possibly be, we assumed it was people in the next building. I never told Marsha that I was already familiar with this arguing couple. But once or twice a week, this couple would argue and we would both hear it. Loud and hateful bickering became a common sound. It took us a long time to realize that these arguments always lasted precisely the same duration, and was most always the exact same content and tone. We eventually did recognize that it was as if a record was being played...over and over. Eventually, I caught on. It only took me a few trips to the porch to realize that when I approached the back porch, it would stop abruptly. Whatever the purpose of this "performance," it was aimed at us.

Within weeks, we fell into a slump. Marsha confined herself to her kitchen for eighteen hours a day, and I worked all day, returning home to spend my evening hours in the basement. For the first time in our marriage, we argued regularly. I would seek refuge in my basement. I continued to smell the fresh burning wood and would check the old pot belly stove diligently. The newspapers I had planted were always there...never did I find anything burned.

The magazines and clutter were gone, but I continued to talk to *Ben* as if he was there. The basement was now clean and ready to paint. The old smells of coal dust and old papers were gone, replaced by the fresh smell of cleaning solutions and bleach which were used to wash the place down. Yet, from time to time I smelled the overwhelming scent of burning wood. I couldn't figure it out. If one is familiar with coal, the smell is strong and unmistakable. A building that has stored coal and has had the concrete saturated with coal oil, has an odor that is near impossible to get rid of. Yet, somehow, the smell of burning wood would overtake it, with no source of anything burning. Although I thought it made no sense, it actually made perfect sense, given the situation. Not many items remained in the basement as a reminder of the previous owner--except that stove. I felt I was making my mark on the building, yet there was no explanation for the goose bumps or the strange feelings I had while I worked alone in the night down in my basement.

Before painting the basement, I shifted my effort to the garage. It was full of boxes and junk. I didn't bother examining the contents or the items, I just wanted them gone. With the basement, I slowly threw things out in amounts that the garbage men would accept. By now, I was tired of all this junk and my patience wouldn't tolerate throwing it away in parcels week by week. I tracked down the garbage men and made them a deal. In Chicago during the early seventies, this was not a problem. It cost me twenty dollars to get a special truck to visit my garage with two men that would clean it out completely. Little by little, things were getting done.

* * * *

It was mid-January one evening when our door bell rang. I went down the stairs to the entry hall, and there was a woman in her thirties at the door. She introduced herself as a member of the family that owned the building, and one of the heirs involved the in sale. I asked how I could help her, but didn't recognize her from being at the closing. She was definitely not one of the people that had attended the sale.

"Could my husband and I go through the attic?"

At this point, I really didn't know that there was a real attic. I assumed it was a crawl space.

"Why?" I asked.

"Well…er, I…uh, think there may be an old cradle up there that once belonged to me."

I had the distinct impression that she was lying. Not recognizing her, plus the fact that she seemed to be lying, turned my attitude quickly to being rude and abrupt.

"No, I don't think so. But, I'll tell you what. If I find a cradle up there, I'll be glad to call you and let you have it. Would that be okay?" She didn't know what to say, except that it was acceptable. She wrote her phone number on a card and gave it to me. Without another word, she left.

Marsha wanted to know what that was about, and I explained. She didn't understand why I wouldn't let them in. I told her that they had months to search this place before we owned the building and in reality, I didn't know who the hell they really were. Plus, it was obvious that the family had ransacked the place. So I gave Marsha the number and told her to call her if a cradle was found.

I knew I had an attic, but I really didn't know where the entrance was. We lived on the second floor and there was no entrance from inside. I assumed that the there was no access to the peak of the building, which was likely a crawl space. Logically, I went to the back enclosed porch and looked up to the opening in the roof, which was about a two-by-two foot square. There was a cover that matched the ceiling which protected it from the weather.

Dark as it was, I still decided to take a look. I positioned my ladder below the opening and pushed up...the cover easily lifted off. I climbed the ladder onto the roof of the porch, and was facing a small window. Examining it with only a flash light, I could see it was not a conventional window. A fastener at the side held it in place. I unfastened the window and it swung open. I could now crawl into the attic. There was no light switch, so I shined my flash light all around. I could see a few boxes in the center of the attic, which was as far as my flash light could shine without going further in. Goose bumps hit me in a flash. I decided not to go in. I would wait until Saturday, when I could see it in daylight. I won't say I was afraid, only reluctant.

It was about then that I realized that my behavior was changing. It bothered me that I didn't want to go into that attic. I started adding up the things that were abnormal. We had the smell of burning wood, the kitchen door that opened on its own, the phone that wouldn't stay on its cradle, the mixer that flew off the hook, my bath tub stopper, and flickering lights, all unusual. The goose bumps and the feelings that I wasn't alone were becoming more and more frequent. This bothered me. I had lived in many places in my life. Some bright, some dingy, but I never had these feelings before. I had no fear of the dark, and I didn't believe in ghosts. So I was confused by what was happening.

When Saturday came along, I examined the attic. Only a few boxes were there. They contained nothing of importance or value, mostly leftovers of kid's toys, a few marbles, some monopoly money, baseball cards, soldiers and what not. There was no cradle. The attic was made up of the peak of the building. I could walk down the middle, but the walls slanted down as they were at the same angle as the roof. It was clean. There was only one reason to ever come up here and I saw it immediately. Two shut-off valves that controlled the gas for the two space heaters in our apartment. But other than turning the gas on or off for the heaters, the attic was useless, because the trap door was two by two and the window entrance was about the same, only a box would fit in for storage. It made no sense to me other than the architect "goofed." I knew I would have no reason to return to the attic, which was just as well, for certainly I had no desire to be up there.

Our cat was next to react. Kitty clearly claimed the living room as her own from the time we had moved in. A soft velvet chair was her throne. It was late January when we noticed Kitty could be seen fleeing the room, hissing as she left, looking behind as she would run towards the kitchen. The first few times it happened, we would look for Holly, the dog, thinking that maybe the dog was harassing her. But Holly was always by our side and was never in the same vicinity. Marsha and I had Kitty since she was a kitten for four years. We knew her habits and her temperament. Her hisses were deep and resentful, as if she was retreating from a good cat fight. But there was no fight and nothing in sight. Typically, this would happen in the evening and continued for weeks, until Kitty finally abandoned the living room for good. Marsha and I found it curious that Kitty would soon confine herself to the kitchen and our bedroom almost exclusively, but sometimes look at the living room...and hiss on a regular basis.

By February, you could cut the air with a knife, it was so tense. I would come home to, "Eddie, the lights in kitchen were flickering for a half hour. Could you get me a new light fixture?"

I would respond with, "Did you check the phone? I have been trying to call you all damned day."

The cat would hiss, the dog would bark and then the kitchen door would swing open. I was already fed up with the fact that I had to literally watch my bath fill up, or the plug would "pop" out of the drain. When we went to bed, if it wasn't the arguing we heard, it was Holly barking at the "footsteps" on the back porch. At this point, I truly wasn't sure if it was our apartment or the pressures of my job that was causing me this stress. I just knew that something had to give.

Today, you can read this and say, "How did you not know that you had ghosts?" In 2011, this may sound incredible. But in 1970, we were not that smart. There were no movies or books such as the Amityville Horror or The Exorcist at that time. *There were no television programs such as Unsolved Mysteries, or Sightings. The word "paranormal" was a little used term in very small circles. If you look at the ghost movies from the fifties and sixties, that is what we would have expected to experience. If a transparent figure would have appeared, moaning a "Whoo, whoo," we would have known it was a ghost, because that is all we knew at the time. Instead, we found ourselves surrounded by inexplicable occurrences that we initially found more baffling than frightening.*

Each event on its own was not frightening as of yet. Confusing, baffling, yes...but not scary. Had we come face to face with the specter of death, we would have taken a cue and evacuated immediately. But this never happened. It was the little things gradually sneaking up on us and increasing in frequency. One by one, they began stacking up, almost conditioning us to accept them as inconveniences, or just weird happenings. Combined, they accomplished the goal of being totally consuming. We found ourselves from morning to night occupied with our problem.

Marsha and I ceased communicating. I kept my experiences to myself, and she kept hers a secret. But as these occurrences continued to multiply and increase in frequency, it was inevitable that we would eventually discuss our combined suspicions. It was our building, but we were walking on egg shells at all times. There would soon be an event that would cause us to finally open up to discussing our little problems.

"Sometimes if an entity is particularly malignant, prayers, incense and holy water only serve to irritate it and bring about even more violent displays."

Olof Jonsson, The Psychic Feats of; 1971

Chapter Three

Denial

For months, we endured the activity and pretended that our lives and home were normal. Admitting you are faced with something beyond your control is never easy, especially when it inhabits your house. I dealt with the anomalies in my own way, so as to not cause alarm or frighten my wife. She dealt with them not knowing how to deal with my absolute denial. Finally, there came a day when she could not contain herself any longer and the debate began.

"Eddie, I think that this building is haunted." Marsha told me, almost casually, one morning over coffee.

"No way." I quickly replied.

"Eddie, my mixer flies off the wall." Marsha started to build her case.

"So your mixer falls on the floor and that means the place is haunted?" My voice was filled with sarcasm.

"You know what I mean. It's the mixer, the phone, the weird way the pets are acting, not to mention the bath tub...Christ, you have to sit there and watch it fill up or the plug removes itself and wraps around the faucet. What about the kitchen door?" Marsha was certainly correct, as the occurrences were mounting.

I had my suspicions, but failed to admit them, nor would I add my experiences to her list. I guess it was guilt on my part. I felt that if I added fuel to fire by admitting we had ghosts, then how could I say "goodbye" and leave for work, abandoning Marsha to deal with the problem alone? This was especially true because I had no logical explanation. Who could I call, an exterminator? No, I would not admit a problem. Instead, I offered her my logic.

"There is no such thing as ghosts. The mixer falls because I need a bigger hook to hang it on. The kitchen door is old and warped. Who the hell knows about the bath tub? Shit, it's a hundred years old. Maybe the cat knocks the phone off the hook. Marsha, there are no ghosts. I think when crazy old *Myra* leaves, we won't be so paranoid and things will settle down. That's what I think. I also think that you dislike this place. It's old and in the city, opposite to where you originally wanted to live. No, it's not the little American dream house in suburbia, but it's not a haunted house either." In my mind, I was hoping all this would just go away.

"Come on, Eddie, you know the kitchen door should stick closed, not open freely on its own. You have seen the phone come off the hook when the cat was in the kitchen and what about Holly, barking at the 'footsteps' on the porch? You can't just ignore it." Marsha was disgusted and upset.

"Baloney. I'll put a new trip lever in the bath tub, and that will fix that. I'll put a new door in the kitchen and that will fix that. Anything else?" I was in total denial.

Marsha responded. "Well...you put a new light in the kitchen and that didn't work. The lights still flicker for no rhyme or reason? Why do you think replacing things will work, when it hasn't worked yet?" Marsha was chipping away at my theory.

"All you want to believe is that ghosts are the cause of all this crap. I have not seen any ghosts--have you? I don't want to talk about it any further."

I really didn't, because I had no solid explanation. I knew that these occurrences were not normal. Yet, I couldn't understand exactly what they were. Not knowing anything of ghostly behavior made me completely ignorant. Why would a ghost move a hand mixer? Or, unplug a bath tub? I imagined that a true ghost would materialize and scream or moan, trying to scare the hell out of us from the beginning. I figured that real ghosts would come floating across the room in a haze, like some kind of bogey man from a nightmare. My vision was wrong, for I pictured a Hollywood nightmare, not what our real nightmare would resemble.

Keep in mind, that we had no reference for true paranormal activity. There were no cable shows on haunting, nor was there anything in the media even semi-educational. All we had were the ghostly examples of Hollywood movies, which were fairly tame and near humorous. What we were experiencing was completely foreign to our knowledge and perception of what a ghost, or ghostly activity, might be.

I left for work thinking that I had to come up with a solution. Then, it occurred to me. I would call the priest. I would ask the Father to completely bless the building. His last visit was interrupted by the breaking of his holy water dispenser, which seemed to rattle him. I attributed his hasty exit to him being embarrassed and nervous. I would call again.

At about 9 A.M., I dialed the church.

"Father *Barnes*, please." I waited.

"Hello," he answered.

"Father, this is Ed Becker. About two months ago you christened my daughter and visited my apartment?"

"Yes," he answered.

"Well, if you remember, you never finished blessing the building and I wondered if you could come over and finish by completely blessing the building." There was a long silence.

"It...It is not necessary..." he replied, curtly.

"You don't understand Father. If you think back, your holy water dispenser broke and you left without completing the ceremony. I would just like you to completely bless the house. It would make us feel a lot better." I was being naive in thinking that he needed a reminder of the incident.

"Mr. Becker. The blessing I gave will suffice. There is no reason for me to return." His answer was cold and removed.

"Father, I...I don't know exactly how to say this, but...I think there is something going on that makes it important for the building to be blessed." I was afraid to say the "G" word.

"Mr. Becker, I truly don't understand." His tone was unfeeling and uninvolved.

"Father, we know that at least two people have died in that building and we are afraid that...that maybe little things that seem to happen could be...uh...uh, well, because it needs to be blessed." I was doing my best to avoid the issue.

"Mr. Becker, I am busy. If you feel you have a problem, I am not sure who you would call. As far as I'm concerned, the building was blessed." This was to be his final word on the subject.

"Father, may I ask candidly why you seem reluctant to bless my building? Why don't you want to return?" I was getting upset.

"What? What do you mean?" He was sounding indignant.

"Father, I'm a Catholic. I was an altar boy. I know the church. It's no big deal to visit a house twice for a blessing, if for no other reason than to make us feel comfortable. It's just not a lot for a parishioner to ask. Years ago, the priests walked the neighborhood and visited the parishioners regularly. Please, just as a favor for us as parishioners...will you, Father?"

"No. As I said, it is not necessary. I can't help you. Goodbye Mr. Becker." Father *Barnes* hung up the phone on me.

I sat and thought about his first visit. What if it was not a coincidence that his holy water dispenser broke? What if he left because he was frightened? My suspicion was that the good father did have a reason for not wanting to return to my home. I needed to confirm that fact, so I redialed his number.

"Hello, Father *Barnes*," he answered.

"Father *Barnes*, this is Ed Becker again. I hate to bother you, but I would like an answer on this...is my house haunted?"

"Excuse me?" He acted surprised.

"Father, I get the impression that you ran from my building two months ago because you sensed something. Did your holy water dispenser break? Or, was it broken by something? Is that why you won't return?" I held my breath waiting for his answers.

"Mr. Becker, I...I don't know what you mean." He was clearly trying to avoid lying.

"Father, you know exactly what I mean. Were you chased out? Do I have ghosts?" I blurted out the dreaded "G" word.

"I would rather not discuss it. It is something the church doesn't get involved in."

I clearly understood what he was saying. He would not confirm it, but couldn't lie and deny it.

"Father, what am I to do?"

"I cannot help you Mr. Becker. There is truly nothing I can do, even if I wanted to." His voice was wavering.

"If not the church, then who?" I was puzzled.

"Please don't call me about this again. This is not a subject that I can get involved in. I cannot help you. Goodbye." He hung up the phone a second time.

Could it possibly be? Did we really have ghosts? I sat and thought about the day of the christening. Father *Barnes* was going to stay and have lunch with us. He lifted his hand with the brass holy water dispenser and it shattered. Brass does not shatter easily and certainly not spontaneously. The priest then became unglued. He was nervous, sweating, and anxious to leave. He literally ran out and clearly he was frightened. Why? Even if there is such a thing as ghosts, I couldn't believe he would be that frightened. A mixer falls off the wall...so what? The phone comes off the hook...so what? This was just not scary stuff.

It was my logic at the time that the priest seemed to be more frightened at the prospect of ghosts than the average person. After all, anyone that spends his life preaching about heaven and angels would have the ultimate fear of the opposite--ghosts, demons and hell. I, myself, had no fear...only confusion. Thinking back to my religious training, the word "ghost" was never mentioned in their teachings, other than the Holy Ghost. Why? Was it because ghosts don't exist? Or, was it that the church had no method of dealing with them? I needed to talk to someone, so I decided to bring up the issue every chance I had with my friends and associates, feeling out their beliefs on this taboo subject. I wasn't convinced as of yet, but I would start to explore the possibility.

Today in 2011, I view it as a complete hypocrisy that most Christian faiths preach of angels and devils as being real, yet if any member of their congregation claims to have seen either an angel or devil, they will be ignored or recommended for psychiatric help. If one truly reads the New Testament, Jesus expelled demons on many occasions. It is recorded that he taught his disciples to do the same and even sent them out to do this work as one of their primary responsibilities. Ironically, it is a task that our current religious leaders have abandoned. Conspicuously absent is any Catholic reference to earth bound spirits or ghosts.

That evening when I returned home, it was crazy old *Myra* that met me at the entrance door.

"I'm moving out this week, you know?" She said with a sneering grin.

"Yes, I do know." I replied.

Marsha heard me enter, and came down the stairs to greet me. She was at the foot of the stairs, waiting for me to finish my conversation with *Myra*. *Myra* continued.

"I'm glad I'm leaving. I was tired of you coming into my apartment at night and moving things. I know you came into my apartment. You put the cigarettes out in my coffee cup, didn't you?" She waited for my response.

"*Myra*, I never came into your apartment, nor did I put any cigarettes in your coffee. I don't know what you are talking about." I assumed this was just insane delusions.

"I know you were there. You moved my table and chairs. All the time, the same thing, all the time, and the cigarettes in my coffee cup made me mad. You are a son-of-a-bitch for doing that. I'm glad I'm leaving. Now it's all yours...all yours. Hah." She slammed her door.

I looked to Marsha in confusion. I was met with the same expression. Neither of us had the slightest inkling of what she was upset about. Moving her furniture? Putting cigarettes out in her coffee? 'Good riddance,' I thought. I had my fill of the old lunatic. Marsha felt overjoyed that this crazy, unpredictable old hag would be gone in a few days. We decided to put the ad into the paper early. *Myra* would be gone during the weekend and it would take another weekend to clean the apartment up enough to show potential renters. We would advertise the availability as of March 1st.

I decided not to tell Marsha about my conversation with Father *Barnes*, as it would only add to her fears. Instead, I called my friend, *George*. Our conversation went something like this...

"*George*, what would you say if I told you my building is haunted?"

"Ed, I would say that you are nuts. Why do you think that your house is haunted?"

"You know the problem with trying to call here with the phone always busy? Well, sometimes the phone is lifted off the hook. We find the receiver lying next to the phone...all the time." I waited for his comment.

"Ed, get a new phone. Why? Do you think that ghosts are using the phone?" He was laughing now. "That's a good one. You have a haunted phone. What else?"

"Forget it. Maybe when you come over next time we can talk about it. I just wondered if you believe in ghosts."

"No way. There is no such thing. I don't want to talk about it." *George* now was serious.

I was curious. "Why? Why won't you talk about it?"

"I don't believe in ghosts. I don't want to believe in ghosts." *George* closed the door on the subject.

I dropped the issue. I understood what he was saying. By admitting that he believed in ghosts, it opened a door to an element of fear of the unknown; a world which one has no control over. Not believing was safer and more comfortable. We continued our conversation, but talked about other things.

The next day at work, I took my break and sat at the same table with a four older employees. They were in their late fifties. I brought up the subject of ghosts. Only one person laughed. The others considered it a serious subject. The other three all had stories to tell about ghostly experiences in their lives. One told of a house that her parents owned that was haunted. Their ghost was a man that died in the house. At one time or another, each of her family had seen him walking the halls in the wee hours of the morning. She explained that every so often, he would even make sounds. Sometimes footsteps could be heard, other times a murmur, as if someone was mumbling to themselves.

She told of how her family was frightened at first, but how they came to accept the ghost and even ignore him. I asked if the ghost ever approached anyone in her family. She stated that his appearance was always at night, in the hallway and at a distance. On every occasion, it was already dark and his silhouette was normally mistaken for another member of the family. The night she saw him, she thought it was her father. The ghost was moving toward the kitchen in the front of the house. As she passed her parent's bedroom, she could see both her parents sleeping soundly. When she looked again in the opposite direction...he was gone.

She told of how it was impossible to move out and sell the house during the depression, so her parents had the house blessed and learned to live with the ghost. She said her father sold the house in the late forties and to her knowledge, the ghost was still there. Our coffee break was over but we continued the subject at lunch and one by one each told their true ghost stories. Each tale was very believable. There was no talk of screaming banshees or skeletons floating across the room; only very conservative stories with a common thread of people who had died, whose spirits were still walking the earth--as if trapped in this dimension.

As I listened to the stories, I grouped the common denominators in my mind. All these accounts were of people who had died at the residence where the ghosts appeared. My problem seemed the same. All the stories had the ghosts doing different things, so there was no common formula that the ghosts followed in their activity. Each ghost had its own personality it seemed. My story would have fit right in. In at least two of the accountings, the houses were blessed, but it did no good. This seemed to be the case at our building.

I continued my research on an ongoing basis. I asked anyone and everyone about their belief in the supernatural. To my surprise, I collected many stories. Some were first hand accountings; others were handed down, almost like family heirlooms. Much to my surprise, ghost stories were fairly common. I started to believe that maybe--just maybe--such a thing might really exist.

* * * *

Myra finally moved out. I wasn't sure who moved her, but we assumed it was her family. She left hysterical. She was screaming and crying as they led her away in a car that followed the truck with her belongings. As always, the tiny dirty poodle was attached to her shoulder. I watched her staring at the building as the car pulled away. The first floor apartment was finally vacant. *Myra* was moved out on a Saturday, so I had the following day to clean the place out and prepare it for painting the next weekend. Marsha was much relieved to not have that crazy woman in the building any longer.

I didn't enter the apartment until Sunday morning. Except for garbage and litter, it was empty. I was happy that there was no junk or furniture to move out. With all the lights turned on and burning brightly, and with the sun shining through the front windows...it was still dark and gloomy. Because the apartment building was wedged between two larger buildings, I assumed it was because no light could enter the side windows, and the gloom was the result. It was like a cave, with the sun shining through the front window as an entrance.

I started in the front room, sweeping all the litter toward the rear. It accumulated as I swept. Off the front room was the entrance to the first bedroom. The room was darker than the other rooms, and cold. I immediately got the chills when I entered. Being February and cold outside, it was my assumption that somehow the heat couldn't travel to this room. I swept quickly and got the heck out of there. I can truthfully say it was the first time I got the "willies." I just didn't like that room. Throughout the day, whenever I had to go near it, my adrenaline would rise, as if I anticipated a conflict. It was an automatic reaction that I had no control over. It was as if my fight or flight switch would turn on.

Finished with sweeping and cleaning up the debris, I scrubbed the wooden floors by hand. It was at that time that my eyes started playing tricks on me. The first time, I was in the dining room scrubbing when I saw a figure out of the corner of my eye that I assumed to be Marsha, checking in on me. What I glimpsed was in the front room, near the entrance door. With the sun shining in from behind, the form was clearly defined...or so I thought. As I looked up to greet her, it was gone. It was so prominent, that I rose to my feet and checked the front door. There was nothing. I was left rubbing my eyes, thinking that I was seeing things.

Room by room, I scrubbed the floors and washed the walls. I went through bucket after bucket of water mixed with disinfectant soap. I was in the kitchen late in the afternoon when my eyes played tricks on me again. As I was washing the walls, within six feet of where I was standing, a figure passed by the doorway which separated the kitchen and dining room. Again, I saw it from the corner of my eye as I was facing the door at an angle. This time I didn't mistake the figure for Marsha, as it was much taller than her five foot height. I tensed up and faced the door. I said, "Hello?" There was no answer. I walked into the dining room and there was no one. I slowly opened the bathroom door...and there was no one. I shook my head. Surely, I was seeing things. I wrote it off to being overtired. By the end of the day, the place was clean and ready to paint. I wasn't anxious, but I would return the following weekend.

Marsha had already gotten responses from our ad for the apartment. This was a new experience for the both of us. This time we were the landlords, looking for the best tenant. One thing was for sure, we would not discriminate against people with children! Marsha said she had talked to a nice young woman that sounded anxious to see the apartment, even before it was painted. She and her husband had just had a baby and needed to move for the same reason we had to move; their existing landlord didn't want kids in his apartments. Because of their plight, we liked them even before we met.

In the middle of the week, on a Wednesday evening, they stopped by to see the first floor apartment. Though not painted, they liked it. It was large, having six rooms, and was convenient to his job, which was only a mile away. *Dave* and *Ellen* became our first tenants. They left us with a security deposit of one month's rent, plus the first month's rent in advance. Having made them fill out an application, I accepted them, providing their references checked out. I gave them a copy of a one year lease pending approval. Tentatively, they would move in March 1st.

Marsha was happy that we had rented to a young couple. I tried to explain to her that they were tenants and this was not a social relationship. I wanted her to keep her distance. It was imperative that the landlord-tenant relationship be maintained. I understood that it would be difficult to collect or raise the rent on someone that had become your friend. Worst case, how could you ever evict your friend, should that become necessary? She promised that she would do her best.

The next morning I tested my bath tub once again. I intentionally put the plug in as tight as I could, then I went into the kitchen for my morning coffee. Minutes later, entering the bathroom, as usual, the plug was dangling from the faucet. I vowed that this was the last time. I was working for a plumbing supply company, so when I went to work, I asked for help. One of the old timers explained how to put a new trip lever on my old tub. I wanted the kind that has the little handle that you move up and down so the metal plug closes and opens. I bought the most heavy duty drain plug they had.

I spent the evening installing the trip lever. I could hardly sleep, waiting to try it the next morning. At 5 A.M., I was up like a shot. Entering the bathroom, I pushed the handle and plugged the drain. I adjusted the running water to the right temperature and went for my morning coffee. I could hardly wait to check the water. I finished my coffee and a cigarette and then held my breath as I entered the bathroom. The bathtub was full! The new trip lever was the solution. I quickly called for Marsha to view the results. I stood there like the conquering hero.

"See, I told you so. I fixed it." I was gloating.

"Well, we'll see," is all she could reply.

"This is, Ed, one; Ghosts, zero." I was rubbing it in.

"Are you going to replace the whole damn building, wall by wall?" Marsha made a comment that would hold a lot of truth and would echo in my mind at a later time. It would not be as easy as putting in a new drain to eliminate the rest of our problems. I would learn that they did "own" the entire house.

Though basking in my victory over the bath tub, I left for work pondering my other problems. I had no solution for the telephone coming off the hook. It was a new phone, and in fact, a new phone line, so what else could I replace? The hand mixer was new and was ours prior to moving in, so why was it being moved all the time? It was my assumption that now that *Myra* was gone, so would the "footsteps" on the back porch. The smell of burning wood in the basement was the only item to which I had a possible solution. I would merely remove the old pot belly stove. But, this was not urgent, for it was a manifestation that Marsha was unaware of and the smell didn't bother me; it was more a puzzle to solve.

It may have been my "solution" of replacing the old drain plug that aggravated the ghost in the bathroom. Although I had no more problems with the tub, the activity in our apartment increased, as if I had disturbed the balance of things. I came home that evening to a wife that was frightened and anxious.

"Eddie, all day the animals have been going nuts." This was her greeting.

"Like how?" I asked.

"Kitty keeps looking toward the front room and hissing. Holly normally sits with me all day quietly, but today she started barking and looking toward the front door as if someone was there. It wasn't just a bark, it seemed a warning. A half bark, half growl type of sound. I was worried, so I kept Christine in here with me all day." As Marsha spoke, I sensed a legitimate concern. This was the worst feeling I could possibly have, and that was the inability to protect and provide security to my family. I felt my best strategy would be to fake denial.

"You know, *Myra* is gone and there is no one here. The animals must be hearing sounds from the outside. Maybe it was a utility man walking around. What am I to do? I got the dog as a companion and watch dog, but now if she barks, it worries you more than not having a dog in the first place." I had already been through a hell of a day at work, being involved in a computer conversion. This just was not the greeting I had expected.

"Eddie, these animals spend their day walking on egg shells. If a pin drops, Kitty jumps in the air and Holly starts growling at nothing. It makes me nervous."

"Then let's get rid of them. If the animals become an aggravation, I have no tolerance for it. I'm busting my butt at work and I come home to the world's biggest remodeling project. I have no more time to solve the animal's nervous problems. Let's just eat."

After dinner I returned to the basement. I had told the new tenants that they could use it for doing laundry, and I wanted it as clean as possible. I was in the mood for an easy task, so I decided to paint the concrete floor. I could pour the paint and simply spread the paint with my brush, giving the floor a thick coating. It would have a week to dry before the new tenants moved in. Taking a break from time to time, I wondered about this building and its history. I knew *"Ben"* had died in our apartment and based on what I had found in his shed, he was a sick man, mentally. There was no doubt that *Myra's* mind was completely gone. I had questions. How many other lunatics lived here? How many other people died here? I remember sitting in total silence as I heard a piercing sound.

It came from directly overhead. It was the sound of a table or heavy chair being dragged across the kitchen floor. Although loud and immediately overhead, I was not alarmed. I knew there was no furniture in the first floor apartment and that no one was there. I studied the sound. I could almost picture a single person dragging a heavy wooden table and the legs bouncing on one side as it moved. Impossible! Having painted the floor surrounding the stairway up to the first floor, I could not get to the entrance. I proceeded out the door into the yard and up the stairs onto the porch where I looked through the kitchen window. Of course, there was no one there. I reasoned it was Marsha on the second floor and that the sound carried through the vacant apartment.

Later that night, I asked her.

"Did you move any furniture in the kitchen this evening?"

"No." She stated.

"Think about it. Did you move the table to mop the floor or anything like that?" I needed a solution.

"No." She was now curious. "Why do you ask?"

"I just thought I heard some noise up here while I was down stairs. No big deal."

It was a big deal. I went to sleep thinking about how distinct and close that sound was. I was starting to believe. I still had no fear, as I regarded the possibility a novelty. So big deal...I had ghosts...so what? Marsha, on the other hand, was coming apart. Being totally involved in my career and obsessed with fixing up the old building, I was too busy to consider her feelings. All day long she spent her time in the apartment watching as lights flickered, checking the phone to see if it was off the hook, and sometimes dodging her hand mixer or replacing dishes that moved. Plus, listening to sounds and calming the pets as they went crazy, barking and hissing from time to time. She was becoming a nervous wreck. The affection and closeness that we shared was changing to hostility and indifference. This barrier had set in without either of us being totally aware of being manipulated. We were becoming the "arguing" couple.

* * * *

Our new tenants *Dave* and *Ellen* had moved in. It felt good to have the first floor occupied. *Dave* worked for a security company, while *Ellen* stayed home with their newborn. The sounds of people living downstairs became a comfort almost immediately. Now, when we heard furniture move, or a door slam, or people talking, it was assumed to be our tenants. But it would be only a week before the first occurrence on the first floor.

It was a Saturday afternoon when *Dave* caught me returning home from work. "Mr. Becker, could I talk with you?"

Dave was short, no taller than five feet, with dark, long hair. His eyes looked huge, as they were magnified by his thick glasses. I answered, looking down at him. "Sure, but do me a favor. Call me Ed." At twenty four years old, I did not feel like a "Mr." as of yet.

Dave looked concerned and uncomfortable. "Could you let me know the next time that you turn off the electricity? You see, I was playing my favorite album when my record player went dead. If you could, I would appreciate it." I could tell he was bothered by the incident.

"When did the electricity go dead?" I was puzzled.

"It was yesterday evening, at about 8pm. Everything went black, as if the power was shut off completely. It was like someone just threw the switch."

"I'm sorry, but I know nothing about it. You and I each have our own electric boxes. I can't think of a reason why I would need to do that. It must have been the electric company."

"That's what I thought, but I looked up on your porch and your kitchen lights were on, so I knew you weren't affected. I assumed you switched off the first floor for some reason. It went back on after a few minutes." Now he was puzzled, but I could tell that he had his doubts.

"*Dave*, if it happens again, let me know. I have had a few electric problems in our apartment. What can I say? It's an old building. If it happens again, I'll call someone in to look at it." I believe he sensed that I knew more than I was telling. He thanked me and we went our separate way.

As weeks passed, we became aware of the fact that their relationship was not the best as we would hear them arguing from time to time.

Being April, the Chicago winter was over and with clear streets, I took to coming home for lunch a few times each week. It was a warm, bright Monday, and after driving home for lunch, I saw her for the first time. It was an old lady sitting outside on my front stairs. She was dressed in a heavy coat, and appeared frail. As I pulled the car to the curb, I studied her.

I assumed she was either visiting my tenants, or was a near neighbor from the building next door.

I bounded up the stairs and said hello as I passed her. She looked to be about eighty. I passed her at arm's length. She smiled, a motherly warm expression in return, as an answer to my hello. She didn't speak, but I understood her smile. Entering the apartment, I immediately asked Marsha, "Who is the old lady?" To which Marsha professed no knowledge. "What old lady?"

"It's nothing, no big deal." I replied. I just wasn't all that curious.

In Chicago, it was common in the old ethnic neighborhoods for people to sit on the front porches or stairs. For an old person to take a walk, then rest their bones on the steps of a building was not unusual in any way. When I was a small child, I would walk miles with my Grandmother through the neighborhoods while she shopped at various stores. We always rested by sitting on the steps of some apartment building for a few minutes, and then continued our journey home. Therefore, I didn't even think about it as being unusual. Leaving for work, the old lady was gone.

* * * *

It was in April, as the weather turned nice, when I met *Walter*. *Walter* owned the beautiful, brown, three story brick building next door. He was in his late sixties. He greeted me as we passed in the back yard. I was taking garbage to the alley and he was grooming and preparing his flower beds, as his yard was a vast flower garden.

We introduced ourselves and he invited me over to chat. I jumped the low chain-link fence into his yard. *Walter* was a likable old guy. He reminded me of my grandfather. Gray haired and stocky, I could tell he was once a laborer. His handshake was firm; it was like shaking hands with a tree stump. He invited me into his basement, offering me a chair. I looked around to find it immaculate. Unlike the natural gas space heaters in my building, *Walter* still had an old boiler, which he fed every morning with wood.

With the boiler door open and flames going strong, it held the same appeal as sitting near a roaring fireplace. *Walter* smiled as he produced a new bottle of Southern Comfort from behind his neatly stacked pile of wood, and just happened to have two shot glasses. He filled each and handed me one. "Nazdrovia," he stated with feeling, as we downed the shot. I can still remember that it was 10:30 in the morning. I knew right away that if there was something good about owning this building of mine, it would be *Walter*, my new neighbor. There was great chemistry between us from the beginning. As he poured us both another shot, I knew he had found his drinking buddy, and I had found my key to the building's past history.

Within minutes, the alcohol hit my blood stream and I was void of proper etiquette and quite relaxed. I found out quickly that *Walter* and his wife *Stella* had owned the brick building for nearly forty years. He knew the whole history of the neighborhood. I slid smoothly into asking him questions about my apartment building. He started by telling me about the mother.

"She died of a broken heart, you know." His smile faded.

"No, I don't know much at all." I responded.

"One of her sons lives just down the block from here. He walks by every day, going to and from work. *Bob* is his name. He had a falling out with her and moved. He never spoke to her again. As she grew older and was confined to a wheel chair, she would sit looking out the front window. He would pass by twice a day and never give her a glance. The bad feelings went on for almost twenty years, and not a word was spoken between them. They say that she would sometimes call to him through the window. Even if he heard her, he never looked in her direction. He ignored his mother right up until the day she died. She died of a broken heart, they said."

"Did...did she die in the apartment?" I asked, tentatively.

"Oh yes, on the first floor. She had another son that also died in that apartment. He died in the front bedroom. He was very sick. Not physically, but mentally...in his head. He was some kind of deviate--crazy. He died young, in his twenties. There was a mystery surrounding his death. Supposedly he died suddenly, and there was a rumor that it was actually a suicide. I remember that boy; he had a crazy look about him. We all knew he wasn't right in the head."

"Who else died in that building?" I asked.

"*Ben's* wife. She hung herself in the basement. That's where they found her. I saw them bring her out; it was sad...very sad. That truly was a suicide.

They said she went down there to do the laundry, and never came back up. *Ben* found her. She was a nice enough woman, but they never got along. They were always yelling at each other." As *Walter* spoke, I could tell that the tragic events surrounding the building had affected him. "*Ben* was wrong. He grew up in that house, then married and stayed there with his family. He should have moved out...got a place of his own...it might have been different."

"*Walter*, I get the impression that this family had a history of mental illness. *Myra* was completely insane. If the younger son and *Ben* were also mentally ill, I assume the father may have been ill in some way." I was probing further.

Walter and I had shared three shots of Southern Comfort. Both of us were pretty well primed. *Walter* was now becoming more candid. "Oh, him. Yeah, he was real bastard. He abused the whole family. He was mean, and not a very good person. Now that I think about it, he may have also been a sick man. They never found his money when he died. They said he kept it in old coffee cans and buried it somewhere. He also owned some land in Indiana. They dug the place up and even broke the concrete in places in the basement. No one ever found a penny. He built that house, you know?"

"No, I didn't." I answered.

He studied me. Then spoke. "You are the first person outside of that family to own that building. Come to think of it, you are the only person, besides *Ben's* wife, to live there outside of their bloodline." He looked worried. Having had the alcohol, I was also candid.

"*Walter*, would you think I'm crazy if I told you that...that strange things sometimes happen in that building?" To my surprise, he didn't even flinch.

"No. I would be surprised if you told me otherwise. My wife and I saw you move in. *Stella* was very concerned that you and your wife were so young, and with a baby yet. We felt sad that you bought that building. We know that they are still there. They all lived their lives in that house. All the kids never left, except *Bob*. They spent all their time in that building, and two of them never even married. They lived their lives and died in that building. I would be careful." He really looked concerned.

"How were they as neighbors?" I asked.

"They kept to themselves. They never said hello, or even Merry Christmas. They never took care of the place, as you well know. *Stella* and I were glad to see you fixing it up. You sure have a big job ahead of you."

Walter had given me a lot to think about. It was time I left. He poured a final shot of Southern Comfort and hid the bottle behind his wood pile. "Nazdrovia," and we hoisted the last toast. "I'll stop by again." I assured him.

"You tell your wife that she can always come and sit with *Stella*, if she feels like...like...she needs to get out for a while." I thanked him for the offer and jumped the fence back into my yard. I would not tell Marsha about this conversation. In total, there were five deaths, with two being suicides. I strongly felt that one of the suicides may have been a murder. The way *Walter* presented the death of the young son as mysterious, along with the way he stated, "They said it was suicide," left me wondering if that younger son, who was so disturbed, wasn't just killed. My mind was a blur. Relative to what I had learned about ghosts, this building certainly fit the profile. I really didn't want to confront the issue, for the facts were in favor of a problem that logic couldn't solve. I decided to take a break from the place.

I went up and got Marsha and the baby, and we left for the rest of the day. We went shopping and then stopped at my friend *George's* to visit. It was about 10 P.M. when we arrived home. I parked in the garage and we entered the back porch. Moving past the first floor, our tenants were in the kitchen and could see us pass as we went up the stairs.

Dave came rushing out. "Have you been gone?" He asked. "Yes, we have been gone since this afternoon. Why? Is there a problem?"

Dave's expression was one of complete confusion. "There was a lot of racket up there. I thought you guys were having a big fight."

"What kind of noise?" I asked.

"It was mainly in the kitchen. But there were some big crashes in the front room." He looked at me as if I was lying, and possibly too embarrassed to admit that we had a problem.

I groped for an answer. "Maybe it was the damn dog chasing our cat around. Did you hear any barking?"

"No, we just heard crashing, like someone throwing furniture around.

It sounded like something heavy dropping and being dragged around." He was still in disbelief.

"Well, thanks *Dave*. I appreciate you guys watching out for us." We proceeded up the stairs and into the apartment. As I turned on the kitchen light, I called out, "Holly, here girl. Kitty, here kitty kitty." Everything was in place. I walked to the front door, and it was locked. Everything was in order. Looking into our bedroom, I could see the dog and the cat sitting together, cowering in the corner. Holly wagged as I approached and Kitty gave me a familiar "meow" as she rubbed up against me. I asked, "What the hell is wrong with you two?" It's funny how you talk to pets as if you expect them to answer. In this case, I believe they would have had a real interesting story to tell.

It was the very next day that I had trouble calling home. As usual, the phone was busy. I knew it was off the hook. I decided to drive home for lunch. Pulling up to the building, the old lady was once again sitting on my stairs. I noticed she was dressed almost exactly in the same manner as I last saw her. She smiled pleasantly as I passed within inches of her on the outside steps. Again, I said, "Hello," and again, she only smiled. She had warm, dark eyes, and the look of a loving grandmother. As before, I was not in the least curious about her presence. Maybe she was a neighbor that was used to visiting or just sitting there.

Over lunch I asked Marsha about her, and Marsha's response was the same. She had never noticed her. We walked to front room window, where I pointed down to show Marsha who I was talking about, but once again... the old lady was gone. "No big deal," I thought. Why would Marsha even notice anything on the front porch when she spends all her time sitting in the kitchen?

* * * *

It was a night during the week in early May when I finally broke down and confided in Marsha that I believed we had ghosts. It happened spontaneously while we were in bed, about to go to sleep. All the lights were out when Holly jumped from the floor to the foot of the bed and stood in an attack position, growling. Attack position for a husky is back arched forward and neck to the ground, protected. The hair on her spine was standing straight up and her growl was deep.

I could see her bare teeth in the dark, as she stared growling at the open doorway. A sliver of fear ran through my body as I prepared for confrontation. I had faith in the dog, as huskies are rarely wrong. I jumped from the bed and switched on the light. Holly followed behind, growling all the way. There was nothing to be seen, at least by me. I knew Holly had "seen" something. Whatever it was, was foreign and possibly threatening, for I had never seen Holly react in this way before. She was prepared for a fight to the death.

I turned off the lights and returned to bed. Holly slept on the bed at the foot. She had now calmed down.

"What was it?" Marsha asked.

"I think she saw something or sensed something that we couldn't see." I blurted out, honestly.

"You think she saw the ghost?" Marsha asked.

"Yeah, I think she saw something that she imagined to be threatening, that we just couldn't see." I was tired and with my adrenaline pumping, it took me a second before I realized that I had just admitted my new found belief. I expected an "I told you so," from my wife, which would have been well deserved and long coming. Instead, Marsha put her arm over me and kissed my neck. "Good night," she whispered. I went to sleep telling myself, "This is my house...my house."

"My experience with ghosts does not bear out that all of them were sudden death victims, but nearly every case indicated the entity was emotional--either fearful, hateful, or anxious about the manner of their deaths."
"Most commonly, ghosts felt they had left things undone."
Joseph DeLouise, Psychic Mission, 1970.

Chapter Four

Playing With Ghosts

"What do we do now?" I asked, while sipping my morning coffee. It was the first time since owning the building that Marsha and I would talk openly about our ghosts.

"I don't know, but I wish we could sell this place." Marsha was quick to produce an answer that she obviously had been contemplating for some time.

"You know that's impossible. We have no equity. We would lose money, because we would pay real estate commission. More importantly, we have no money to buy another place. I don't see the problem as anything other than an aggravation. So big deal, the phone comes off the hook...so what?"

"Eddie, we don't know what it will do next. From the time we moved in, it's been one thing after another. You saw Holly last night; she sensed danger."

"Look, I'll admit that something...something is here, but it's not like the bogey man for Christ sake. This is our house and I don't care what it is--it's out of the question. We will move in good time, but not because we're afraid of something that 'might' happen. Remember, even if we wanted an apartment, where would we find one that would take a child and pets? Face it...we have our backs to the wall on this one. These ghosts are going to have to put up with us for a while."

"Eddie, I feel that it is testing us. I think it knows when we get aggravated and it does these things on purpose. I think it senses our fears and will escalate those things that it knows will scare us. I think it will do what it has to do in order to eventually chase us out."

"Well, I'll tell you what I think. I think old *Ben* is just stuck here and doing the things that he did before he died. He lived alone here. Yeah, he picked up the phone, took a bath, and used the kitchen, which is exactly what he is doing in the afterlife. So what?" I looked up and asked, "Isn't that right, *Ben?*" Marsha was stunned.

"Don't do that." She scolded.

"Why? If he is here, why not talk to him?"

"It really doesn't bother you, does it?" Marsha questioned.

"Well, if you mean, am I afraid? The answer is no. This is my house. If *Ben* is here, he can stay because I don't know how to get rid of him. Don't make more of this than it is."

"Eddie, doesn't it bother you that he is here watching us?"

"No. Old *Ben* is harmless. He doesn't watch people; he looks at pornography and girly magazines...Don't you *Ben*, you old deviate." I was again chiding *Ben*.

"God, don't do that. What if he gets mad?" Marsha was worried.

"Here I am *Ben*, take your best shot...see? He is air...nothing. Come on *Ben*, put up your dukes. See? Nothing. Don't start coming apart at the seams because you picture a ghost as some kind of 'Frankenstein monster.' We are real...*Ben* is not. I think that's quite a big difference. Believe me, if I felt there was a real danger to you or Christine, we'd be out of here in a flash. I don't see it. He's a bag of air--nothing more."

I was totally sincere in the fact that I really didn't see a threat. In admitting there was a ghost, I had found it a novelty. I never noticed the effects the ghost already had on our lives. It had created tension in our marriage. It had Marsha walking on egg shells; afraid to turn around, for fear of facing the "grim reaper" or some skeletal specter. It had me totally occupied with justifying everything that was unexplained with some logical answer. I didn't see the obvious. The ghost had moved into our lives in a big way. It dominated our emotions, thoughts, and conversation. Whether we admitted it or not, we lived in anticipation of the next display of ghostly activity.

* * * *

That evening as Marsha and I ate dinner, the door between the kitchen and dining room swung open with force. I commented, "*Ben's* here." This was normal activity that was not unusual in the least. This time, I carefully studied the door. There was a little metal loop that I had screwed into the door frame. The loop was there for the hook on the gate that we used to keep Christine from crawling out of the kitchen. That little loop was at about the same height as the door knob. I decided to put a crimp in our ghost's behavior. I jumped up and quickly found a strong piece of string.

I then closed the kitchen door tightly. I tied the string to the loop and wrapped the balance of the string around the door knob. The door was now tied shut. Marsha had been watching me intensely. I turned and announced my expected victory.

"Take that, *Ben*," I announced. "Let's see him open the door now."

As we continued eating, our attention was focused on the door. After only a few minutes, the expected happened. The door knob turned slowly and the door moved as if to swing open. But it didn't, for the string held it shut. We both watched as the door bounced and vibrated faster and faster. It could only move the distance of the few inches of string. After a few minutes, it stopped.

I couldn't resist. "What's the matter *Ben*? Door stuck? Tired? Sorry *Ben*, we want the door closed."

I looked to Marsha. "I'll make you a bet. I'll bet the phone comes off the hook in the next ten minutes. Old *Ben* will want to do something to get even." I was laughing as I continued eating my dinner. When finished, we finally opened the door and checked the front room telephone. Sure as heck, the phone was off the hook. I went to the front room and replaced it, laughing all the way. In my thinking, dealing with a ghost was no different than dealing with a child.

I announced to my next solution to Marsha. "If he keeps that up, I'll install a second phone in the kitchen and disconnect the living room phone. Then, we'll leave it there for him to play with. I'll fix that old deviate." I was having fun. This was now becoming a game to me. However, it was a game that would dominate my life.

The phone rang. It was *George*. "What the hell were you doing on the phone for the last hour?" He asked.

"I wasn't on the phone. It was off the hook again."

"Oh yeah, the ghosts did it." He was making fun of me.

"Well, if you don't believe it, come on over and I'll show you." I said it with confidence.

"Show me what?" *George* was curious.

"I'm serious. I can get the ghost to open the kitchen door. You have to see this." I was excited.

"So I come over there to see a door swing open? Big deal." *George* was not impressed.

"No. Opening the door is not the trick. What I do is tie it closed so he can't open it, but he tries and tries. The door bounces back and forth...it's amazing. Come on over. You really have to see this."

"How about tomorrow night? *Ann* can drive me over and we can talk for a while. Then I can see this stupid trick." *George* didn't like the "G" word.

"6:30?" I offered.

"You're on. Later." He hung up.

I turned to Marsha. "*George* and *Ann* are stopping by tomorrow night... okay?" I asked.

Marsha was agreeable.

"I can't wait to show *George* the kitchen door." I stated.

"Eddie, you're just going to make them mad." Marsha scolded.

"Them? You believe there is more than old *Ben*?" I asked.

"Yes...yes, I do. I believe we have more than one ghost in this house." Marsha spoke with authority.

I didn't confirm her comment, but knew she was 100% correct. After learning of the family through *Walter*, I wouldn't be surprised if we had four or five ghosts. I knew the mother and father had both died here, plus two sons and a daughter-in-law. All in all, there were at least two deaths on each floor and one in the basement.

The next morning we awoke freezing, as the apartment was cold. Marsha woke me up while wearing her heavy robe. I asked, "Why is the heat off?"

Marsha had no clue, but said that the space heaters were off. I assumed that the gas company had turned off the gas for some reason, like doing work in the street, which would have shut off the pilot lights in our space heaters. I immediately went to the space heater and tried, unsuccessfully, to turn on the pilot light. "Are all of them off?" I asked.

"No," she answered. "The one in the front of the house is fine, and the gas stove is working. It is only this unit."

"Strange? It is like the gas is turned off..." As I said it, it struck me. The valve for each of these space heaters was in the attic. The curiosity was too much for me, so I went to the porch and up the ladder, opening the access door and climbing to the roof. After entering the access window, I could see clearly that the lever on the valve was in the "off" position. I made my way over and turned it on while scratching my head. Going back downstairs, I lit the pilot light and on came the heat.

Marsha had one of her "I told you so" looks on her face.

"Don't even say it." I ordered.

"Well, someone is trying to get your attention. These things don't shut themselves off."

It worried me, but I refused to show it. "It could have been a pressure-type thing." I stated. Actually it could not, because of the simple lever design of the valve, but how would she know? "All I know, is if it keeps up, I'm moving the valves into the damned kitchen!"

"Why would it keep up?" Marsha replied, in an all-too-sarcastic way.

"Because shit happens!" I refused to discuss it any further.

* * * *

The pressure was off and I had found my freedom. I would not keep the secret any longer. I had ghosts. I would admit it to myself and anyone else that would listen. I started talking to my coworkers about my problem. To my surprise, most of them listened intently and were very interested. Only a few thought it was unbelievable.

As usual, I had trouble reaching my wife by telephone. The line was always busy every time I dialed. So I drove home for lunch. Once again, the old lady was sitting on my steps. I parked my car at the curb and dashed up the stairs, saying "Hello," as I passed her. She smiled warmly and nodded, but didn't utter a sound. I thought nothing of it, except how frail she appeared.

"Is old *Ben* at it again?" I asked Marsha, walking into the kitchen.

"Yes. The phone was on and off the hook all day. Holly has been doing nothing but barking and Kitty is hissing up a storm. I can't take it anymore." Marsha appeared exasperated.

Quickly I grabbed her hand. "Come with me," I told her as I led her into the front room. "Look out the window...this is the old lady that I was speaking of."

Marsha looked out and down at the front stairs. No one was there. She looked back at me and asked, "What old lady?"

"Don't tell me she's gone?" I replied as I looked out.

Sure as heck, the old lady was not there. From the second floor window, I had a clear view of the street. I saw no one coming or going. If she did disappear quickly, she must live close by, I reasoned.

"Well, I'll show you next time. Let's have lunch, because I have to get back to work."

* * * *

That night, *George* and *Ann* came over to visit. We sat in the kitchen, catching up on the activities of all our friends. All the while, I was waiting to unveil my ghostly trick. Finally, after much conversation, the time was at hand. *George* finally asked, "Well, what are you going to show me?"

Although *George* was blind, I spoke to him as if he could see. It was unspoken that he would "feel" or "sense" whatever was happening, and *Ann*, his wife, would see for him and explain. I rose slowly and completely closed the kitchen door that led to the front of the apartment. I then took a piece of string and attached it to the loop attached to the door frame, tying the other end around the door knob. If the door opened, it would only open an inch, for that was all the tolerance the string would allow.

I walked over to the table and sat down.

"Now, we'll just wait until old *Ben* opens it." I announced.

"Oh, now you have a name for the ghost?" *George* questioned sarcastically.

"Yeah, I call him *Ben*, because that was the guy who died in this apartment. He is the one that had the old porno collection in the basement shed."

"Tell me about the porno collection," *George* asked.

"It was a weird collection. There were literally hundreds of magazines going back decades. Not real pornography, just movie magazines and a few nudist magazines. There was nothing raunchy. The sick part, was all the shoe boxes containing clippings. Whether it was a photo from the newspaper or a cartoon, if it showed a woman depicted in a sexy position, he cut it out and saved it. There were literally thousands of them all neatly stacked in old shoe boxes. Oh, I did find a few of the first Playboy magazines, which are probably worth something."

We all sat around the kitchen table, which was more or less in the center of the room. We continued to talk. Nothing happened, and I was becoming impatient. I called out to him.

"*Benny*...come on *Ben*, you know you want that door open. Come on out *Ben*, you old deviate." I began mocking him.

"Eddie, don't...don't." Marsha pleaded.

"What's the matter?" *George* asked.

"Marsha thinks that I'm antagonizing him." I answered.

"Boy, you guys are both nuts." *George* mumbled.

I continued to taunt him. "*Benny*, you old deviate, open the door. I know you can do it. Come on, you old pervert."

As I was talking, the door knob started to turn.

Ann exclaimed, "Oh *George*, I can see it. The door knob is turning!" Her eyes grew to the size of silver dollars.

I sat there grinning as the door started to open, but wouldn't, for the attached string limited the distance it could move. We watched as the door bounced against the string but wouldn't open. The whole time *Ann* was describing the ongoing events to *George*. It continued for about two minutes. Then, it was over. The door stood motionless.

"Well, what do you say to that?" I asked.

Ann was speechless, but *George* was quick to comment.

"I don't believe it. So the door opens or vibrates...so what? That doesn't mean anything. That's no proof that a ghost exists. It's all bullshit, if you ask me." *George* wasn't convinced. He continued his skepticism. "Some lame ghost you have. Big deal. He can vibrate a door. I don't believe it. It could have been the vibration of a truck driving by. Anything could cause that. Let's see him really do something." *George* was not impressed.

About four feet behind *George* was a cabinet, which was about eight feet tall. Since the ceiling was ten feet tall, there was a space between the top of the cabinet and the ceiling. To fill that two foot space, I had solidly attached some spindles, and behind the spindles were plastic plants, giving it a trendy "garden" look.

As *George* continued his comments that ghosts didn't exist, we were treated to a display of ghostly energy. One of the spindles detached and traveled about six feet overhead to the center of the table, pausing in mid-air. As we noticed it and glanced upward, it came crashing down to the center of the table. It fell from the ten foot height, but didn't bounce. It was like someone slammed it to the center and held it from bouncing with force. With a loud crash, it sat where it landed. As *Ann*, Marsha, and I stood speechless, *George* could only flinch at the sound and ask, "What the hell was that?"

For what seemed like minutes, no one spoke. I took a deep breath. "I guess I pissed old *Ben* off...or you did."

George, being blind, reached out to feel the spindle. In doing so, he realized that had it landed on one of us, it could have easily done some physical damage. *George* recognized the sound of the force of which levitated the spindle. He had me guide him to the cabinet from where the spindle originated. Even being blind, he could judge that the distance from the cabinet to the center of the table was beyond what would be a distance that was within a normal fall range. He was now impressed.

"I don't know what did this, but I still don't believe in ghosts." This time, *George*'s comment had a strong sense of insecurity.

George quickly decided it was time to leave, and *George* and *Ann* never came to visit us again. Although he never admitted to believing in ghosts, he was reluctant to spend time at our apartment any longer.

* * * *

It was Memorial Day weekend when my younger sister, *April*, and her family came over for a backyard barbecue. During that visit, I mentioned our ghost. My sister was very interested. A student of the occult, she had been using Ouija boards and studying the paranormal for many years. After listening to our tales of ghostly activity, she literally begged me to move in.

"If your first floor tenants move out, I want the apartment. If there is any way you can not renew their lease at the end of the year, do that for me. I have to live here!" *April* was excited.

"Well, I think you're nuts! This has become nothing but an aggravation. Shit moving around and sounds with no physical source…it's not that funny. Who knows what these damned things will do next?" I answered.

Her husband, *Jim,* didn't believe in ghosts and would not have any of this nonsense. He would go along with moving in, if that is what my sister wanted. I assured her that if the first floor tenants moved out, she could have the apartment. She had two sons; *Kenny*, age three, and *Roger*, age two, so the three bedrooms would give them much more living space. At the time of my commitment, I truly did not see the danger. I only saw *Ben* as my private clown, not as the tortured soul he likely was.

*   *   *   *

I made it habit to come home for lunch regularly during the week. I frequently would see the old lady sitting on my steps. I always smiled and said "Hello," as I bounded past her. Her gentle face always smiled back, but never did she speak. By the way she sat on the steps, with her legs folded awkwardly, I developed the impression that maybe she couldn't walk, or was somehow handicapped. If so, how did she get there? How did she leave? I always was looking for where she lived, but never found out.

You must understand that this image of an old woman appeared as solid as you or I. There was nothing that hinted at the slightest, that this possibly could be a ghostly apparition.

It was early one morning when leaving for work, that Marsha finally saw the old lady. As I exited the front door of the apartment, Marsha called to me, "Eddie, kiss me goodbye."

I stopped on the landing at a point where the stairs turned downward and had a view of the lower hallway and entrance. Marsha came down the few stairs and kissed me. It was at the moment that we became aware that someone was standing at the bottom of the stairs, watching us. She appeared suddenly at the base of the stairs and was looked directly up at us. It was the same old lady that I had seen so many times sitting on the outside steps. Unlike the gentle smiling face I was used to seeing, this time she had a serious and almost painful expression. She slowly turned away and glided out of view toward the entrance to the first floor apartment.

"That's her." I explained to Marsha. "That's the old woman I see sitting on the outside steps all the time. Hold on a second." I motioned to Marsha to stay put. I walked to the bottom of the stairs, and she was gone. As I looked around the corner--there were only the two doors. One led to the outside; the other to the first floor apartment. I looked up to Marsha.

"That explains it," I announced. "She didn't go out the front door, because we would have heard it open and close. Therefore, she must be staying with *Dave* and *Ellen*, our tenants. I'll bet she's the mother of one of them. She probably came out to get the paper." I waved goodbye and felt confident that the mystery was solved. How could I have not realized that the old woman only started to appear after my new tenants had moved in? Of course she belonged to them, what other explanation could there be?

That evening over dinner, Marsha laid a bomb shell on me. I sensed her serious mood.

"Eddie, *Ellen* doesn't know anything about the old woman."

I was in shock.

"No old woman is staying with them?" I didn't believe it.

"No. *Ellen* looked at me like I was nuts when I asked her"

I thought a second. "You saw her, right?" I began doubting my own vision.

"Yeah, I saw her..." Marsha said solemnly.

"Well, we know she didn't go out the front door; it never opened and we would have heard it open or close, for it makes way too much noise. She had to go into the first floor apartment. Where the hell did she go?" I was perplexed.

Marsha took a hard swallow. "Eddie, I think we saw a ghost. I think you have been seeing one all along. She isn't real."

"Marsha, I saw her. I was close enough to touch her many times. She can't be a ghost...she looked solid...real."

"What does a ghost look like?" Marsha asked. "You are the one that told me not to be afraid of the Hollywood ghost images. We have never seen a real ghost before. How do we know what they appear like?"

"I admit we have a ghost, but it's likely to be *Ben*, the guy who died here. Who the hell would that old lady be, his mother? Now we have two ghosts, one on the first floor and one on the second floor? Give me a break...there has to be an explanation."

"Eddie, you knew she didn't live next door in the brick building and you know that she doesn't live in the abandoned store or the apartment on the other side. So now explain it? How else could she leave this morning without using the doors?"

I was still in shock, babbling my same logic. We had seen a ghost, but it wasn't scary. She didn't float, and she wasn't transparent.

"But...but...she didn't look like a ghost. She looked solid. She was as solid and real as you and I. I have seen her up close...she was solid...I could have touched her. You saw her?"

"Yes, yes...I saw her." Marsha was assuring me that I wasn't hallucinating.

"I'll tell you what...next time...I will reach out and touch her...I will. Next time she's on the front steps, instead of walking past, I'll grab her hand...I will."

I meant every word of what I had said. I already pictured it in my mind as I spoke. I could see myself driving up and seeing the old lady sitting on my steps. I would smile and jump the stairs two at a time as normal. In mid-flight, I would say, "Hello," and reach out and grab her arm. The only part I couldn't picture is whether I would grab on to something solid, or be left holding...air. The ghost of the old woman must have been aware of my thoughts, for she never appeared on the front steps again. She never allowed me to get within arm's reach. I would only see her once more... from a distance.

* * * *

The next weekend, I looked for *Walter*. When he surfaced, taking out the garbage, I jumped the fence into his yard.

"*Walter*, please I...I really need to speak with you."

"Sure Ed, how can I help you?" We walked together to the alley. As he put the garbage into his can, I was asking him an important question.

"The old lady that we spoke of, the one that sat in the window beckoning to her son, what did she look like?"

Walter knew immediately why I was asking. He looked concerned.

"She looked like any old woman. She looked old and gray and frail in her later years. She was about 5 feet tall, or so, and she was barely a hundred pounds." There was a question on his face, but before he could ask, I asked him a few more.

"How did she normally dress? How did she wear her hair? What color were her eyes?" I was asking questions in machine-gun fashion.

"She normally was overdressed, as if she was cold all the time. She sometimes would sit on the front steps in a wool coat, even though it was warm out. Her hair was long, but pushed up in the back; she never let her hair down. Her eyes were dark, probably brown...dark brown, I think."

He continued to describe her, but I wasn't hearing him. I had heard enough. I knew that I had seen her many times and could likely describe her in much better detail than *Walter* could ever remember. I blurted it out. "I saw her, *Walter*."

To my surprise, *Walter* hardly raised an eyebrow. He thought for a second, and looked me directly in the eyes. "Be careful." He stated.

"She didn't try to scare us or anything," I offered. "She just appeared on the steps and in the front hallway."

"She was a good woman as far as I know, but if the others are there, be careful." He looked worried. I told him that I would be surprised if they weren't there.

He thought for a second and then spoke. "Yes, she used to sit on the front stairs when the weather allowed, and before she became wheel chair bound."

"Thanks *Walter*, I just needed to know." I started to walk away.

"Wait, Ed...did you call for a priest?" he asked.

"Yes...yes, I did. I called him, but he wouldn't help me. Father *Barnes* is who I talked with."

"Go see him, Ed. Visit the rectory, talk to him in person. The church will help you." *Walter* sounded so sure that the church was willing to help.

He called to me as I walked away. "Come over and have a shot with me later." *Walter* yelled as I hopped the fence. I nodded in approval and waved goodbye.

I went immediately to tell Marsha of the old lady.

"Marsha, it was the mother that we saw in the hallway. *Walter* described her to a tee."

"Eddie, now you sound excited, as if we have won some sort of prize. I'm scared. I don't know what they will do next. I want to go home."

"What? Home?" I sat down.

"I need to get away for awhile. Can I take Christine and go home to visit my mother?" Marsha was pleading.

"I...I don't understand?" I was in shock.

"Eddie, I need to get away from this place. I'm going crazy here. Ever since I had the baby, I've been locked up here, all day and all night. I never get to leave. Please...please? It's not all that expensive."

Marsha and I had not been apart since we met, so this suggestion was quite a surprise. I didn't like the idea, but I understood it was necessary. We agreed that I would make the reservations for her to fly home to Tulsa. She intended on staying a week. There was no discussion of me coming with her, as it was understood that my job was far too demanding.

In a few days I would be driving home from the airport alone. For the first time in four years, I had to fend for myself. Coming home to an empty apartment didn't bother me. I knew it was haunted, but still had no fear. All I felt was a strong sense of domain. It was my building...not theirs. I was greeted at the door by my pint sized tenant. *Dave* was anxiously awaiting my return.

"Ed, the electricity went on and off twice last night. Is there anything you can do?" He looked up at me in utter frustration.

"I'll call in an electrician to take a look at the lines. I'm sorry." I was at a loss to explain it. "I just got back from the airport. I...I'll call tomorrow."

"Yeah, Marsha told *Ellen* she was leaving for a week or so. We kind of expected it...with you guys arguing so much lately." *Dave* said this as a matter of fact.

"Arguing?" I questioned.

"Well, I'm sorry, but we could hear you almost every night."

I didn't want to tell him the truth, that what he was hearing was the same sounds that Marsha and I have heard since we moved in. I avoided any explanation. "See you later, *Dave.*" I was sure that *Dave* and *Ellen* had heard the arguing, but it was not Marsha and I they were hearing. I proceeded up to the apartment and Holly greeted me at the door. "Well, we're on our own for a while girl."

It was on this first night of Marsha's absence that I had a whole new experience. After returning home, I sat in the front room listening to music. I was feeling sad at the circumstances that drove my wife to leave home, searching for an escape. It was about nine o'clock in the evening when I felt a little hungry, so I went to the kitchen and opened a can of soup. As I poured it into the pot, Holly started barking, and it was her 'alarm' bark. She was running back and forth across the kitchen, barking frantically. I set the pot on the stove and turned to Holly.

"What's the matter girl? Need to go out?" She continued barking. I grabbed her leash, attaching it to her collar, and led her out the back door. We patrolled the yard, and then walked down the alley. After about ten minutes, Holly was calmed and we proceeded back. Upon entering the kitchen, I could smell something burning. I looked to the stove and the gas burner was turned on and my soup was smoking. I ran to the stove and shut it down. I knew there was no way I had left it on, because I had never turned it on in the first place. I realized that this was a dangerous display, and unlike *Ben* to do this.

"*Ben?* Did you do this?" I asked. "*Benny,* this isn't funny, you old fart." I scolded him. Holly stayed at my side. I was no longer hungry, so I set my alarm clock and went to bed. Holly and Kitty joined me and within minutes, I was out like a light.

Near 2:00 A.M., Holly was standing at the foot of the bed, growling. It was her deep, threatening growl. Kitty was in the corner of the room hissing. I awakened with a start. I could see the light in the kitchen, shining into the bedroom doorway. It took me a second to realize that the light shouldn't have been on, for I had turned off all the lights before retiring. I slowly arose, making my way to the kitchen. It was empty and dead silent. I sat in the kitchen, smoking a cigarette, wondering how I would end this nonsense. There had to be a solution, but none came to mind. I switched off the lights and returned to bed.

The next morning, my loneliness set in. There was no hand to stroke my head and awaken me; instead, the sharp sound of an alarm clock shocked me awake. There was no cup of coffee awaiting me, and instead, I had to make my own coffee. After taking my bath and dressing, I walked Holly and packed my attaché for work. I then went to the kitchen door and to the key rack. My keys were gone. '*Impossible!*' I thought. I always hung my keys there, but this time they were nowhere in sight. I checked my pockets. I went to the bedroom and checked the top of the dresser...no keys. I retraced my steps from the previous evening, but no keys were to be found.

I paced across the kitchen, trying to figure out where the keys might be. As I walked near the sink, I could see my keys lying in the drain. I picked them up and examined them. I immediately recognized that the key to the garage had been bent in a near perfect "L" shape. Though the key was bent at a 90 degree angle, it wasn't broken or cracked. Years later, Uri Geller would do this same thing using telekinesis; but for now, this was the first time I had witnessed this phenomena. I was at a loss to understand why the garage key? It was a new lock and a new key, with no link to the past. It should mean nothing to the ghost. It simply made no sense.

Once at work, I took the key into the shop and asked the foreman to straighten it for me. He did so slowly, using a vise, and then taping out the final kink with a hammer. He never asked how this happened and I never offered an explanation.

At the end of the day, I again went home to an empty apartment. The phone was off the hook when I entered, so I put it back on the receiver. Holly and Kitty were huddled together in the kitchen, and both were glad to see me. I carefully hung my keys on the key rack near the back door. I put Holly on a leash and took her out the back door for a walk.

Coming down the back stairs, *Dave* met me on the first floor. "Mind if I walk with you?" he asked as he petted Holly.

"Not at all." I replied.

As we walked, *Dave* talked freely of his background.

"I'm part Indian you know." He stated.

"No, I wouldn't have guessed." I answered.

"Well, I have a touch of French, but I'm mostly a Canadian Indian."

He did have the dark hair and features of a French Indian. He looked at my right hand with interest.

"Bad luck," he exclaimed, in a most definite voice.

"What?" I asked.

"The ring on your finger--it's bad luck."

On my pinky finger was a black star sapphire.

"My people believe that a black stone breeds evil spirits." I could see he was dead serious. He began telling me the history of the Indian superstition. As he spoke, I could only think of how he would react if I laid the ghost story on him. I didn't.

At this point I knew that talking about the ghosts would be taboo. Prior to his comment about the black stone, I was going to tell him that it wasn't Marsha and I that he had heard yelling during the past week. I made small talk, but was thinking about how fast he would pack up if I told him about the problem. As he talked about his Indian superstitions, my eyes darted left to right down the alley, looking for what I feared…bad people. Ghosts were not my fear. Although stuck with a troubling problem, I found *Dave* naive of the real dangers of the city.

His assumption that Marsha and I were having relationship problems, made him candid about his own marital problems. I listened to his troubles as we walked. The one fact that stood out in my mind was the fact that his problems seemed to begin only after he moved into my building. I wondered if it was a coincidence. I decided to talk with his wife, *Ellen*. If she knew about the ghosts and it was causing tension, she surely wouldn't tell *Dave* because of his superstitions.

We had soon made the rounds of the neighborhood and were back in our yard. I said good night and took Holly upstairs. Coming in the back door, I glanced at my keys…still on the rack. I made a sandwich and spread my work on the kitchen table. I sat, debugging computer programs, until late that night. When I couldn't keep my eyes open any longer, I went to bed.

The next morning I went through my normal routine, until I went for my keys…which were, once again, gone. I looked first to the sink. They weren't there. I searched frantically every nook and cranny. There were no keys to be found. I was becoming angry. I started cursing *Ben*.

"You son-of-a-bitch, where are my keys?" I looked in our drawers and on the cabinets. I looked under the table and in the garbage can. Searching and swearing, I covered every inch of the kitchen. Finally, reaching up high above the dish cabinet, I felt my keys. I pulled them down, and again, the garage key was bent in the exact same manner...a perfect "L." This time, I tried to straighten it with my hands. It was a big mistake, as it broke into two pieces. I was still upset and swearing at *Ben* as I left for work.

My opportunity to speak with my tenant, *Ellen*, came at lunchtime when I returned home. As I let Holly into the yard, she came out to say hello.

"*Ellen*, you got a minute?" I would get right to the point. "Have you had anything strange happen since you moved in?" I queried.

"Like what?" She seemed to ask innocently.

"I don't know," I responded, "but like the electric goes off from time to time. Is there anything else happening? I...I mean like-"

"I know what you mean. Like footsteps on the back porch at night? Or my dishes crashing to the floor? How about the inside basement door opening all by itself after it's been locked? Is that what you're talking about?" She was very serious.

"I take it you haven't told *Dave*?"

"No way. He would be moving out in a second. He's part Indian, you know; very superstitious."

"I take it that you know that we possibly have a ghost?" I stated.

"Possibly? Possibly?" She was smiling. "Ed, I knew it after the first week. I just wasn't sure if you knew. I thought maybe it was only the first floor that was haunted."

"Are you frightened?" I asked.

"Not yet. So far, it just is an aggravation, except for the plates that broke. It likes to move our chandelier in the dining room. My grandmother had a ghost in her house, so I'm not that scared. But *Dave*...he would move out in a second. I don't talk to him about it."

Ellen had an innocent smile. She was a young, at nineteen, but she looked no older that sixteen. She had long, straight brown hair, with innocent blue eyes.

"How long can you keep a secret?" I asked.

"I'm not sure. Maybe if I can talk to you and Marsha about it, it will be better. Sometimes I get agitated and have no one to talk with about it. A couple of times I almost blurted it out."

"Well, when Marsha gets back, come up and have coffee with her. You can both talk about it. I've got to go."

I took Holly back to the apartment and headed back to work. That evening, I was immersed in thought about my ghosts. I was sure we had more than one. I knew that the old woman was down there, but *Ellen's* comment about the breaking of dishes didn't sound like the work of the gentle old lady that I had seen.

I was truly confused. I spent the evening trying to apply logic to the problem, but in these situations, logic fails to apply. Only months before I thought ghosts were a figment of the imagination; now I was trying to figure out how to evict them. I still felt no fear. It is hard to explain why I wasn't afraid. In retrospect, I should have been. It seemed that each event on its own was not frightening, and maybe that was the answer. I still felt that there was an explanation and a solution to relieving this problem. Going to bed that night, I put my keys under the pillow.

The next day would bring my final appeal to Father *Barnes*. Leaving work at lunch, I decided to visit the church as *Walter* had suggested. Arriving at the rectory just before noon, I asked for the priest, Father *Barnes*. I sat in the office, waiting. I believe he was hoping I would just go away. Eventually, he came to talk with me. I noticed the unwelcome expression he was wearing, as he tried to force a smile and greet me cordially. He sat at his desk, making this a formal meeting.

"Mr. Becker, how can we help you today?"

"Father, I need the help of the church."

"What can we do for you?" he asked, as if he didn't know.

"I really need for you to bless my building." I hoped for an affirmative answer.

"Mr. Becker, we have discussed this once before." His tone was like that of a father scolding his son.

"Father, we have ghosts, I think you know that."

His face became pale as he stood up and walked around the room. He swallowed hard before he spoke.

"Mr. Becker, I have no reason to visit your home. I cannot get involved in this type of thing. The church does not get involved in these matters."

"Father, I don't know what to do. It's driving us crazy; I need the help of the church. Please." I was begging.

I watched him perspire as he paced back and forth.

"Mr. Becker, I told you, the Catholic Church doesn't get involved in these things. There is nothing I can do." He stated flatly.

"Father, I've been a Catholic all my life and an altar boy. I know it is no big deal for you to come and pray for us. I'm not asking for much."

"Mr. Becker, I must refuse. Maybe you need some other type of help, such as a counselor."

I felt my blood pressure rising. I was getting angry.

"Father, I thought that was what the church was for. I have never asked anything of the church in my whole life...only this. Now, you recommend a counselor? What kind of counselor?"

"Mr. Becker, I can only say that I have no authority to recognize or pursue this matter. I hope you understand."

I rose from my chair and glared at him.

"Father, I only understand that you are willing to accept my donations, but heaven help me if I need something from the church. The only thing I understand is that our relationship is a one way street. You never hesitate asking for donations, but now that a parishioner needs just a little of your time, what do I get?"

I could see the relief in his face as I ranted, for my display of emotion gave him a reason to excuse himself. I should have seen it coming. In effect, I played right into his hands.

"I'm sorry, but I must excuse myself from this conversation. I had hoped that you wouldn't feel this way...good day."

He turned and left the room quickly. I never thought I could be this angry at a member of the clergy. I was swearing to myself as I exited the building. I felt alone and abandoned. As far as spiritual matters, the Catholic Church was my only hope in this matter and they had turned me away. This would be the last time I would visit a Catholic church, outside of attending a wedding ceremony or a funeral.

Stopping at the apartment before returning to work, I entered to the phone lying on the table next to the receiver. I cursed the phone and cursed *Ben*. I could see the poor animals huddled in the corner of the kitchen. I was about fed up with this whole business. I needed a break from this affair, and I decided to take one.

I returned to work and immediately asked my boss for the rest of the week off. He could easily tell that I was under stress and quickly agreed. At the end of the work day, I stopped at the first floor apartment to see *Dave* and *Ellen*. I asked them for a favor. I needed for them to take care of the pets and explained that I was driving to Tulsa and would be back in four days. *Ellen* was happy to take Holly in and would stop up in our apartment and feed Kitty once a day. I left them with a set of keys.

As I entered my apartment, as usual, the phone was off the hook. I replaced it, waited a second, and dialed Tulsa. I explained to Marsha that I was packing a bag and would be on my way within the hour. I intended to drive straight through and would be there around 6:00 A.M. the next morning. I had driven this route many times before. I knew it like the back of my hand. It took me less than two minutes to pack. I delivered Holly to my tenants, and was soon on the road.

I will always remember the twelve hour drive. As I drove, my mind was busy; sorting out the facts and exploring possible solutions. I wondered how and why these things existed. What exactly are ghosts? Why do they stay here? How do they materialize? From where do they draw their energy? Is there anyone that can help? Can they be driven out? Questions...questions... but, no answers. Boy, I needed this vacation.

"People expect ghosts to fit into a Hollywood stereotypical image...but they don't. They were once people, and do the normal things that people do. Like you and I, they can deeply resent having their privacy violated."

Edwin F. Becker, 2011.

Chapter Five

Fear Arrives

Dave met us at the door. "I'm sorry Ed, but *Ellen* and I are moving. Here is a written 90 day notice, as per our lease." *Dave* handed me a neatly typed piece of paper, and I didn't know quite what to say. We had just gotten back from Tulsa, and were coming up the back stairs. It was late Sunday night, so I knew they had been waiting up to deliver this notice.

"Can we talk about this?" I asked.

"No. We like you and Marsha, but we have to move." He sounded apologetic.

"Is it something we did?" I asked.

"No, oh, no. It's just that we can't live with this situation."

I knew as soon as he had said, "this situation," exactly what he meant. What I didn't know was whether *Ellen* had told him that the building was haunted, or if something happened while we were away.

"*Dave*, what happened?" I asked.

"It has been a nightmare since you left. It sounded like there was a fight upstairs. We were about to call the police. Screaming and furniture crashing, but no one was there."

Dave almost looked as if he was going to cry. I decided to cut the conversation short.

"*Dave*, it's late. You and I both start work early. What if we get together tomorrow night and talk about this? I won't ask you to stay, I promise. Marsha and I would just like to know the details. Okay?"

"Fine. I'll see you tomorrow night." *Dave* closed his door, and Marsha and I proceeded upstairs. I was apprehensive. What if it wasn't a ghost? What if the apartment was burglarized? I told Marsha to wait on back porch as I went through the apartment and did a quick check. Kitty greeted me at the door. I flipped on the kitchen light and slowly went room to room, checking for anything out of place.

There in the middle of the living room, sat our green velvet arm chair, facing the kitchen. It was a heavy fully upholstered chair, though equipped with casters so it could be moved about. Entering the room, I looked to the telephone, but the phone rested on the receiver as normal. How did my chair move to the center of the room? The carpeting was thick "shag" and all activity would show by the fact that the shag would become matted. Sort of like, foot prints in the sand. I saw no tracks that should have been there. Puzzled, I quickly moved the chair back in place, saying nothing to my wife.

I motioned Marsha in and within a few minutes, we were all tucked in bed. Before I could drift off into sleep, I heard the distinct sound of someone coming up the back stairs with slow, deliberate, heavy footsteps. I could also hear Holly barking downstairs, as we hadn't taken her back yet from *Dave* and *Ellen*. Marsha whispered, "What's that?"

I replied, "It must be *Dave* bringing Holly up. I'll go get her."

I arose from the bed and headed to the back porch. Opening the door, there was no one there. I figured maybe *Dave* had come up and saw that our lights were turned off and went back down stairs. I flipped on the porch light and walked down the back stairs. As I reached the first floor, the door opened and Holly came running out with tail wagging wildly. I bent down to pet her and heard *Dave* say, "See what I mean?" Not knowing exactly what to say, I avoided the question as if I didn't hear him.

"Ed, this has gone on every night. The footsteps are nothing. We heard screaming like someone was getting killed upstairs. Holly was going nuts. I heard your kitchen chairs crashing around the room, right over my head." *Dave* was clearly frightened.

"I don't know much about ghosts, *Dave*, but besides making some noise, I don't think they can do much." I tried to appear confident, not showing the concern that had built up over the past few months.

"I've heard many stories about ghosts doing harm to people. That's why I need to leave. I'm afraid for my family. If I find a place sooner, could you let me out before ninety days?" *Dave* sounded as if he was ready to pack immediately.

"Sure. I wouldn't force you to stay, if you really feel the need to leave. Remember, we're still on for tomorrow night." I took Holly and returned to bed. Marsha asked if there was a problem and I answered that there was not, and it was only *Dave* returning the dog.

Having driven 12 hours and only slept 5, Marsha had a difficult time waking me the next morning. In movements programmed by habit, I went through my routine of preparing to leave for work. My routine came to an abrupt halt when I reached for my keys...they were gone. Marsha was unaware of this new phenomena, so initially I said nothing and proceeded quietly in searching for my keys. At first, I tried to act as if I had simply misplaced them. As Marsha watched, I checked all the normal places that my keys could possibly be. I prolonged my search, trying to lull her into losing interest so I could check the 'out of the way' places. I needed to get to work, so breaking down my façade, I finally began checking the sink and cabinets, reaching into corners and crevices. I must have looked ridiculous.

Marsha definitely noticed. "What are you doing?" she asked.

"What does it look like? I'm looking for my keys." I answered.

"In the kitchen cabinet?"

I didn't answer, but reaching up to the very top of the cabinet, I produced my keys. As I examined them, sure enough, my brand new garage key was bent in the now familiar "L" shape. I handed the keys to Marsha.

"Did you ever see anything like this?" I asked.

"Eddie, this key is bent? What is this?" She was confused.

"This whole thing started while you were away. *Ben* apparently decided that he likes my keys. I was so tired last night that I forgot to put them under my pillow."

"Under your pillow?" Marsha was now more confused.

"I'm not sure, but I think that *Ben* is getting even with me for tying the kitchen door. He hides my keys in the kitchen and bends the garage key into an "L" shape. I've found the keys in the sink or on top of the cabinet every time. I just don't understand the fixation with the garage key always being bent the same way, and always same key. I had broken one key trying to straighten it out, so this one is brand new. It just makes no sense." I was literally scratching my head in confusion.

"I'm scared. I don't like being alone here." Marsha stated.

"Well, the cats out of the bag, so to speak, so invite *Ellen* up here to talk about it. If things were so bad while we were away, she may be scared or want someone to talk with."

Marsha was happy that I allowed her to befriend our tenant. Prior to this, it was my belief the any personal or social contact was wrong. Before I could drive to work, she was already on the phone calling *Ellen* and before Marsha could hang up the phone, *Ellen* and her baby were sitting in our kitchen. It was as if the dam burst, as they traded stories of their experiences over the past five months. Later, Marsha would relate to me that the events occurring in the first floor apartment were similar, but yet entirely different. *Ellen* was eager to share experiences, for she had kept them to herself until this time. Most were even unknown to her husband. They both sat in the kitchen for the whole day relating their personal ordeals. That's where I found them when I returned from work that evening, still sitting in the kitchen, talking a mile a minute. Seeing how relieved Marsha appeared, I would not deny her this relationship with our tenant, as I understood it was short term.

Before *Dave* joined us, there was plenty of time to discuss those events that *Ellen* did not want *Dave* to hear. She did not want to scare *Dave*, as he strongly believed in ghosts and evil spirits. She would share much of her experiences, with most being casual, as far as her perspective...except one. She related her story before her husband joined us.

It was a month or so after they had moved in. In a logical move, they put the baby in the front bedroom and themselves in the back bedroom. She said that this way they could put the baby down early, and still could talk and listen to music without disturbing the baby. She said *Laura* was happy in that room. Being a new mother, she was not totally familiar with a baby's habits. It seemed *Laura* was content with amusing herself for hours alone in the room, almost never crying. *Ellen* stated, that she felt blessed having such a good baby.

One afternoon, while in the kitchen, she clearly saw a man standing in the baby's doorway. She froze, seeing he was much taller than her husband. She watched as he stepped into the baby's room. She ran to the room, reacting automatically without thinking, as any mother would do, but found no one there. She said that she would have thought she was seeing things or losing her mind, except for one thing; *Laura* was looking at the empty corner of the room with her arms extended, as if motioning for someone to pick her up--but no one was there. As *Ellen* watched, *Laura* in her own baby language, was cooing, smiling, and extending her arms as if she saw someone familiar in the empty room.

Ellen had the distinct impression that *Laura* was sharing the room with someone that she couldn't see. Although the baby definitely wasn't frightened...*Ellen* was. There was no way *Laura* would stay in that room another night.

That night, without telling *Dave* why, they moved the baby's room to the middle bedroom. *Ellen* gave *Dave* the flimsy excuse that she felt insecure about possibly not hearing *Laura* cry out. *Dave* thought nothing of it.

After hearing her story, I was very curious as to the description of the man she had seen. I hoped that it would provide me with facts that *Walter* next door would find meaningful. The man appeared under six foot, between 5'9", and 5'11" as best as she could judge. He was lean for his height; almost too slender. She said his hair was a dark brown, and that his face was "distorted," in a manner that she felt was not normal. "Scary," was another word she used to describe his features. Her description was more that he was deformed rather than evil, but abnormal and frightening, none the less. I was anxious to speak with *Walter* to see if he could identify this description as a family member of the previous owners. *Ellen* stated that this incident was the only one that had truly frightened her.

She talked non-stop about the events that she understood to be unusual. Her first experience was with the chandelier in the dining room. One day, soon after moving in, she noticed it swaying on its own. It seemed that as she watched, the movement became faster and more pronounced. It was in a room that was silent and calm, with no windows open, so it caught her attention.

She came to realize that it only swayed when she was in the room or within view. Never did she enter the room to find it already moving. If *Ellen* sat in the front room facing the dining room, it would sway, as if someone knew it was being watched. *Ellen* said she could make it sway as if on command.

Ellen also had a door problem, except hers was with the door that led to the basement. It seemed her door could actually unbolt itself and come completely open. She said this became a source of aggravation between her and *Dave*, because their child nearly fell down the stairs in the walker. At first, she thought *Dave* was leaving the door open, and he thought she was leaving it open. They argued frequently about "who did it," until she realized it continued happening while *Dave* was at work.

She told of how they thought that Marsha and I were having serious marital problems because of all the arguing they heard regularly. They could hear it echoing down the back enclosed porch. It wasn't until we left for Tulsa did they realize that we were gone...yet the yelling continued. She described it as loud and hateful. She said it became louder and more violent while we were gone.

The both of them thought that I was in the habit of throwing furniture around. Frequently they would hear things crash or be dragged the length of our apartment. She said they could almost recognize which piece of furniture was being moved or knocked over. She said any furniture movement was always preceded by a loud startling crash.

Ellen said *Dave* had always thought that I was intentionally turning off their electricity. Since it always seemed to occur while they were playing records, he felt it was my way of telling him to "turn it down." But, he soon found that volume was not a factor. If he turned on the record player, regardless of how low the volume, the electricity would turn off.

I asked her if she had ever smelled burning wood. Her answer was predictable. "All the time, coming from the basement." Again, they assumed that I was using the old wood burner and burning scraps or trash. Their other assumption was that I was in the habit of walking the dog late at night. Since they slept in the back bedroom, it was common to hear someone walking the back stairs. They both heard loud, heavy footsteps, as though made by someone over 6' and 200 pounds, like myself.

Dave soon joined us, and we continued to discuss the problem, although limiting the topics to those that he was aware of, since he held the most fear and superstitions. It was evident that he was frightened. *Dave* was brought up with the belief that ghosts and demons very much exist. He was educated as to how they could be avoided. You never wear black stones, and always wear a crucifix. He was also educated to not interact with ghosts or spirits. He was taught, if a place was haunted, to leave quickly. He was told many ghost stories as a child; stories handed down from generation to generation, which became part of his education and belief system. According to his beliefs, the supernatural was not to be tampered with; it was to be respected and avoided.

Our evening was spent ordering a pizza and shifting the conversation from ghosts to our personal lives. How we grew up, how we met, and how the future would be for our children. I found them to be decent and warm people. I felt sorry for *Dave*, because as the evening wore on, I watched him flinch at common noises and shift back and forth in his chair, as if anticipating a happening. I intentionally left the kitchen door open, so there would be no disturbance by *Ben*. About 10:00 P.M., we called it a night. It had been a worthwhile day for Marsha; just talking about the problem provided invaluable therapy. *Ellen* would become a constant companion, and a fixture in our kitchen for the next ninety days.

* * * *

The next weekend we were called to visit my Aunt Helen. She had committed herself to a full-time nursing facility. It was actually a hospice, before the term became common. After over four years, her cancer had taken its toll. Too weak to care for herself and too proud to burden the family, she knew it was her time to depart. Little did we know she would pass away just two days later. She asked about the building and how we were doing. We were candid about our ghostly problem and began describing all the occurrences. As we talked, she listened intently. Our problem was no surprise to her, as she told us that she was fully aware the apartment was haunted after visiting us on the Christmas holiday. She said that she was familiar with the feeling and could sense it immediately. Marsha and I both didn't quite understand the "feeling." Today, we both have the ability to almost instantly sense a haunting.

Aunt Helen told us a story about a time when my grandparents had rented a haunted apartment and how the blessing by the church did absolutely no good. Their ghost moved the clothes in the closet, moaned, slammed doors, and frequently would sit on the porch late at night. With the sightings came the evacuation of the apartment by my grandparents. Aside from my grandparents, my mother, aunts, and my uncle had all seen the ghost. It was my Aunt Helen that finally communicated to me a theory that I have come to believe. She stated you simply cannot get rid of ghosts. Aunt Helen said that I could get many books at the library that would tell of ghosts that have been around hundreds of years, never leaving. They go about their activity, regardless of human presence. Sometimes, they ignore us if we're lucky...and other times, they may use us by feeding off our emotions, gaining energy.

My aunt stared at my bare neck, as I had my shirt open. In her most serious tone, she stated, "Buy a crucifix, have it blessed, and wear it." She saw that Marsha was already wearing one, so I could tell that my lack of fear bothered her. "Don't stimulate them by giving them too much attention," she warned. Marsha gave me that "I told you so," look.

When asking her advice on my alternatives, it was simple. "Sell, and sell soon." I told her that I really didn't feel the situation was that threatening at this time and I needed a few years to get my money out of the building. Still, she maintained her opinion and kept repeating, "Sell." At the end of our visit, after kissing her good-bye for what would be that last time, she handed Marsha a paperback book and whispered, "Read this." The book was a new tale of horror..."The Exorcist." In a just a few days, I would be looking at Aunt Helen for the last time at her wake.

Returning home, we found Holly hiding in the kitchen, but no Kitty. We called out, "Kitty...here Kitty-Kitty," to no avail. Marsha completely panicked. Frantically we searched the apartment. We searched under beds, behind the couch, but still no Kitty. Marsha started to cry, as if anticipating the worse possible conclusion. Our bedroom window was open about twelve inches, and this was not unusual and was normal. Kitty never went near it, yet somehow I was drawn to open the window and look down. As I looked down, I held my breath, for there was Kitty, twenty feet below on the concrete. I called out, but she remained motionless. I ran out the back door and down the stairs, all the while thinking the worse and wondering what I would say to Marsha. I had this terrible sick feeling throughout my body. Incredibly, when I picked her up, she gave me a familiar "meow," and appeared to not to have a scratch on her. I examined her closely, but there was not a hair out of place. I looked up twenty feet to the window and down at the concrete. "This is impossible," was my only thought. I carried her up the stairs to my hysterical wife.

"Oh Kitty," Marsha cried as she hugged her. We checked her from head to toe and found absolutely nothing wrong. Kitty was an overweight house cat, and not agile as a cat should be. We both knew it was impossible for her to fall from a high second-story window to concrete and survive, much less be completely unharmed. Marsha was the first to speak the obvious. "They threw Kitty out the window!"

"No...No. If Kitty was thrown out by anyone, she would have never survived a fall of over twenty feet down to bare concrete. It's more like they floated her out the window and gently set her down. I...I never have seen anything like it. Look at her! Not a darned scratch. Not a single piece of fur out of place." I was in total awe.

"Well, I think that they tried to kill her. They know that she can see them." The more Marsha thought about it, the more upset she became.

"Marsha, no way. I agree they probably did this, but it must be a distorted message or something. Kitty should have been dead as a doornail and instead, she was sitting directly under the window, as if she rode an elevator down. If they wanted to throw anyone out the window, it should have been Holly, she barks at them all day and all night!"

For the balance of the day, the Kitty incident dominated our thoughts and conversation. Marsha called *Ellen* and asked if there was any noise while we were gone. *Ellen* said it was dead silent. I went to bed that night knowing that as soon as the stores opened, I would be out shopping for a crucifix.

* * * *

A few days later I was wearing my new gold crucifix to Aunt Helen's wake and funeral. The funeral was on a gloomy, wet fall day. At ten in morning, it was dark enough to be five in the evening and the rain was a misty cold spray. When we returned home, *Ellen* greeted us by giving the complete report of the activity and noise made during our absence. "They are real loud today," she said as she followed us up the stairs, carrying her child. As I unlocked the door, *Ellen* looked in, amazed that everything was in place. "I could swear that they broke your kitchen chairs." She said as looked around in amazement.

I had taken the day off of work, so we all sat back and discussed the ghostly activity for the rest of the day. Unlike her husband, *Ellen* was almost amused by what was occurring. We had a lot in common, in that we had no real fear of most of the ghostly activity. When I told her about how I tied the kitchen door shut, she asked me for a demonstration. I refused, because I told her how old *Ben* had bent and hid my keys to get even. It may sound absurd, but we found ourselves laughing. Maybe that was our mistake.

That night, Holly rose to a defensive position at the foot of our bed. Again, she was growling in her deep, wolf-like way. Kitty was hissing in the corner, behind Holly. In the darkness, I could see nothing. Then, she lunged out, as if biting something, and whatever she saw was at the foot of the bed. Chills set in immediately, as Holly lunged forward again, biting at the air. I jumped up and switched on the light. Holly stopped growling, only looking to me and whimpering, as if telling me about her ordeal. I petted her and eventually calmed her down.

"Eddie, this is getting crazy. Please, let's sell this place." Marsha was pleading.

"We've only been here ten months. No way…no way. There has to be a method of stopping this crap. I am not losing money on this deal, I'm not." I switched off the light and we went back to sleep.

Little did Marsha know that I already had been thinking of selling. The problem, was we had no money, and if we sold the building and paid real estate commission, we would walk away with a few hundred dollars. We had bought the building with 5 percent down. Even if sold for the same price, we would pay 3 percent commission, leaving us a mere 2 percent of 16 thousand, or a measly $320 to find a new place to live. I felt trapped.

The next morning brought another surprise. When I let Holly out in the back yard, instead of her usual sniffing around, she immediately took off running. She jumped the back fence effortlessly and took off, never looking back. I chased her until I was out of breath, and then slowly walked home.

I knew why she ran away...she was scared to death of what she had seen and attacked. We never saw Holly again.

As I entered the yard from the alley, *Walter* was waiting. He had just fired up his boiler. "Come here, Ed." he called. I jumped the fence into his yard. "Come sit a second," he said.

"Holly just ran away." I complained.

"I saw. If I see her today, I'll try and catch her for you." He offered.

"*Walter*, did anyone who lived in my building resemble a description of being slender, brown hair, 5'9" to 5'11" and have an ugly or distorted face?" I queried.

Walter's face turned serious, and he instantly produced a name. "*Henry*. He was the son who died mysteriously. He looked like that. His face was always sad; tormented. He died on the first floor...you know, in a bedroom. You saw him?"

"No, I didn't, but my first floor tenant did. I can tell you which bedroom he likely died in. It was the front bedroom. That's where she saw him."

"Did you talk to the priest?" he asked.

"Some priest! He wants no part of this. I know he is aware of the ghosts, but he won't talk about them, or even visit to bless the building. I actually got mad and told him off."

"I'm sorry...I'm so sorry." That was all *Walter* could say. He faded into deep thought. "You know, there are other churches besides the Catholics."

"You're right; the Catholics don't have an exclusive on God, do they?" I asked rhetorically. *Walter* certainly had a point; one that I would think seriously about. I excused myself, as I had to go to work. As I walked, old *Walter* was left sitting by himself, in a trance-like state.

I told Marsha to keep an eye out for Holly in case she returned home, though I knew she never would. Driving to work, all I could think about was my ghosts. So far with the mother, *Ben*, and *Henry*, it seemed we had three ghosts for sure. Hearing the voices arguing, I could clearly identify a middle age man and woman yelling at each other. Likely, one was *Ben's* wife that had committed suicide. She was the one that hung herself in the basement. It was now my assumption that we probably had at least four ghosts. I was at wits end, with no solution and nowhere to turn. I felt helpless. I was now starting to feel fear. Fear for my family and fear for my own mental health. I was starting to realize that my thoughts were dominated almost 24 hours a day by my ghosts. Either I was thinking about what they did, or I was pondering what they would do. My only other thoughts were of how to sell the building, how to get out, or how to rid the building of my unwanted guests. They were controlling my life. There are no words to describe my helplessness.

Fortunately, at about the same time that I was losing hope, Marsha was just starting to look for solutions. Marsha and *Ellen* decided to do some research. Off to the library they went, and they read every nonfiction ghost story they could find. Marsha buried herself in books. She soon found that ghosts have existed for hundreds of years. In this country, records of hauntings began at the time of the Revolutionary war. Going back before that time, are castles abroad, whose ghosts date back hundreds of years more. Graveyards, houses, ships, hotels, restaurants, even highways--all reported to be haunted.

It would be only a few days before Marsha came to the conclusion from doing research that there were specialists to help you with these problems. I had no knowledge of who to call for a haunting. I can still remember the day that Marsha asked me how to contact these ghost experts. I casually told her to "look in the Yellow Pages." I was joking, of course. Little did I know that it was exactly what she would do.

Under Psychic Services, she found two listings for organizations that study such problems. She called the first one on the list, the *Psychic Awareness Group*, and they were immediately interested. After talking to Marsha over the phone, they made an appointment to visit us that same day. When I returned home from work, she gave me the good news.

"I've found someone to help us." She announced. "They are coming over tonight." She was pleased. I was paranoid, not knowing anything about the type of people that would do such a thing and perform such a service.

"How did you find these people?" I asked.

"I took your advice, and used the Yellow Pages. Under Psychic Research, there were two services listed. One of them will be here in a few minutes and they claim they can help us."

"Hey...at this point, I'll try anything. Let's see what they can do." Marsha turned on all the lights and was busy cleaning up when our door bell rang. "It's them." she said, with hope in her voice.

I walked down the front stairs and greeted them, and then led them upstairs. They were a most unusual looking group. The main spokesman was about fifty years old. He was short and stout, with the most unnatural looking bright red hair piece that I had ever seen. It sat on his head, much as a hat would, and was slightly crooked. His name was *John*. With *John*, were three other people. Another man that was very thin and very nervous, named *Tim*. He appeared as though he would rather not be here, and his eyes darted back and forth as if expecting to be attacked by ghosts. He reminded me of the Don Knotts character, Barney Fife. I took notice that he seemed to be in the wrong profession, having such a nervous demeanor.

Then there were the two ladies, both claiming psychic ability. Both were in their forties. One was heavy, and one was rail thin. The heavy one, *Martha*, seemed serious, and was observing and touching everything. She touched the walls as she walked. She ran her hand over the doors she encountered. I could see her "drift" as she closed her eyes from time to time, as if sensing something. The thin one, *Beverly*, did nothing but talk about her ability to "read." She claimed she could read everything from Tarot cards to tea leaves. I listened politely while thinking, "What the hell do tea leaves have to do with ghosts?"

They claimed that as a group, they could help us remove the spirits in the building. Their plan was to set up some equipment in our kitchen to record the evening's events. They intended to conduct a séance and communicate with the spirits. After establishing communication, they intended to merely "ask" them to leave. It sounded much too simple for me, but they appeared very confident. I really wanted to ask them, "What if the ghosts say no?" I was afraid to ask, however, because I sensed that there was no contingency plan on their part.

I watched as they set up their equipment. It was my assumption that they had done this many, many times before. Quickly, they unpacked candles and a crucifix and positioned both on the table, as if fashioning some type of altar.

While the men set up their equipment in the kitchen, Marsha took the ladies on a complete tour of the building. The tour included the first floor apartment and the basement. As Marsha guided them on the tour, I watched the men test their electronics. The gizmos resembled tape recorders that seemed to run at different speeds. One very, very slow, and the other spun super fast. They explained that they could record sounds that were made on frequencies that humans are not able to hear. They had a panel of gauges that would react if something was being recorded, and a needle would designate the frequency. I listened as they made "tech talk" about how they would capture the sounds. Everything was homemade, as the technology was far behind what we have today.

Marsha began the tour in our apartment. She pointed out our problems with the kitchen door and the phone. She took them to the first floor, where *Ellen* took over and pointed out her basement door problem, the swinging chandelier problem, and talked about their electric interruptions. Marsha was most interested in the heavy lady, *Martha*, as she seemed drawn toward the front bedroom. Her arms crossed her chest as she entered. Standing only a second, she came out and whispered to Marsha that the bedroom was "home" to one of our ghosts. She said it was young man, who was very disturbed and had died violently. She stated that this room was very cold. This woman had no way of knowing how accurate she actually was. Marsha knew that *Martha* definitely had a psychic ability. With the completion of the tour, we all gathered together in our second floor kitchen.

John, the spokesman, stated the rules. He closed the kitchen door and asked everyone to be seated around the table. He lit a few candles and switched off the light. He asked everyone to hold hands. One by one, they alternated saying traditional prayers. Since I personally did not witness the psychic display of *Martha* in the first floor apartment, in studying them, I thought that they may have good intentions, but in reality were phonies. I believe our ghosts realized that they were phony, also. As the ceremony continued, I watched the thin man working the recorders. He was sweating and nervous. I could see he was clearly frightened. I think I keyed on him because I knew something was about to happen. I knew the kitchen door would definitely not stay closed.

Upon finishing the prayers, *John* attempted to talk to our ghosts. "You don't belong here," he said in a commanding voice. "You must depart in peace, to your final resting place," he continued.

Now *Beverly*, the "reader", spoke. "We banish you from this house. Jesus Christ commands you to leave." Her eyes were closed, as if she was in a trance-like state. Meanwhile, *Tim* kept checking his sound gauge, looking very, very nervous.

It was at that moment that the kitchen door leading to dining room opened. It started by the door knob turning on its own. This caught *Tim's* attention. Once the knob turned, the door opened with force. That caught everyone's attention, but I was watching *Tim's* face as he realized that no one was there. He stood frozen, staring at the door. His eyes bulged and he stepped back and away as he realized what he had just witnessed.

They were either near the end of their ritual, or they had decided to end the ritual, after the door opened on its own. Everyone in room was silent as the door swung open. It was the ghosts. As if putting on a show, our ghosts seemed to want to show these people they were still there. The spokesman, *John*, asked me to turn on the light. I did so, but within seconds, the lights were flickering. I could see the concern in their eyes. They started packing it up.

As he packed, *Tim* was looking around as if Dracula was about to pop out. I actually felt sorry for him. I watched as they hustled, putting the tools of their trade away in cases. It took them only a few minutes.

As we gathered by the front door leading to the hallway, they explained that we should have no more problems...that our ghosts were gone. Marsha and I were perplexed, for by the sound of *John's* wavering voice, it seemed even he didn't believe his own words. He was anxious to leave and his feet were moving the whole time he was talking. "Nervous feet," is what I called it, and *John* had a very bad case. John was now within ten feet of the telephone, and as he talked, the phone lifted completely off the receiver and hung in the air for what seemed to be a few seconds. It stayed there long enough for all to take notice, and then it crashed loudly on the table.

With that, they swiftly made their exit and said goodbye at the same time. I never saw four people move so fast in all my life. They moved almost as fast as Father *Barnes*. They flew down the stairs three steps at a time. As soon as they were gone, Marsha and I couldn't help but laugh. It seemed comical that the few occurrences that we found common and non-threatening would scare the hell out of so-called experts. When we finished laughing and recapping the evening's events, we realized we were back at square one. That fact was not so humorous.

Marsha told me of the heavy lady's psychic feelings. Marsha, herself, didn't know how accurate she was, for I had never told her the whole background that I had obtained from old *Walter*. It seems *Martha* correctly felt the spirit of *"Henry"*, the son that died in that room. *Martha*, the heavy lady, was for real and did have psychic ability. Over all, it was my opinion that this well meaning group probably had never confronted a real ghost. After leaving our house, they might never offer to do it again. It seemed they were more equipped for a theatric séance than they were for exterminating spirits.

Marsha mentioned that there was one other listing. Illinois Psychic Research would be her next call. I told her to go right ahead. If nothing else, it would be another evening of entertainment.

* * * *

Illinois Psychic Research handled our call a bit differently. When Marsha called, they took her name and address, telling her that someone would contact us in the near future for an interview. Based on the positive results of this initial interview, they would conduct an investigation before taking any action. Unlike the group that had rushed over the same day, Illinois Psychic Research seemed much more selective. We had no choice but to sit and await their call.

In the meantime, I bought another dog, a full grown gray poodle. Princess was already house broken and a good family pet. She took to us immediately. It was her second night with us when the ghosts terrorized her. Princess too, took to sleeping in our room. When threatened, unlike Holly's deep growl, Princess completely went berserk. We awoke to loud, ferocious barking and growling. Princess was standing in the middle of the bedroom, facing the door. Even after I turned on the light, to show her everything was okay, she continued running back and forth in our bedroom, all while growling. It took half of an hour to calm her down.

The next morning, I should have anticipated what would come next. When I let her out the back door into the yard, just as Holly had done, Princess took off in full stride, jumping the back fence and kept on going. In less than three days, we had lost another dog. I looked next door and saw old *Walter* just scratching his head. Marsha wasn't surprised. There would be no more dogs in this building.

It was a Friday evening when Illinois Psychic Research called and said that Tom Valentine would be calling us on Sunday to interview us. Based on the results of this interview, they would decide whether or not to take it to the next level. We had no idea what the next step was, but we agreed. As promised, Mr. Valentine called us on Sunday, and he scheduled a time for us to meet.

At 4 P.M., Tom Valentine was ringing our door bell, and we invited him in. It was a pleasant surprise from the last group. There was nothing strange about Tom. He was a large man who appeared about 30, with a boyish face. He brushed his dark brown hair away from his eyes as he spoke. After introducing himself, he produced a legal sized pad of paper and proceeded to ask us many personal questions. He explained that there are many people that "think" they have ghosts, and he needed to check our backgrounds.

We answered everything he asked. Education, occupation, age, religion, family background, and our personal habits--specifically, whether we drank or did drugs. I was a bit insulted by certain questions, but he explained that he had to ask. Tom was very talented at making us feel comfortable. In a few short minutes, he had us talking about everything from how we met, to what our plans for the future might be. Marsha and I felt as if we had known him for a long time.

I will always remember when Tom asked, "Do you believe in ghosts?" Marsha nodded yes, and I shook my head no. He was amused. This led to a very deep discussion on the subject. I explained that ghosts were not logical to me, but I wasn't sure what else it could be, since none of this was logical. He sensed that I was embarrassed to admit that ghosts might exist.

Tom then told me how he became involved with Illinois Psychic Research. It seems he was with a Los Angeles newspaper, writing a column, when he started research on the subject of ghostly possession. He said that he, too, was not an immediate believer. He told of a visit to a mental institution, where he studied a number of patients with personality disorders. These were typically people that had drastically changed personalities to the extent that they had become someone else entirely. They sometimes even spoke another language.

As he explored their various backgrounds, Tom eventually found common denominators. In a select group that he had studied, he eliminated all the common factors. Family history of mental illness, recent mental trauma, and chemical imbalance had all been eliminated. This left him with an alarming conclusion, and one that would lead him to pursue this interest and even write a book about a nationally known psychic.

His conclusion? There was a common thread that a high percentage of people he studied had dabbled in the occult, or occult-like interests, such as séances, Ouija boards, etc. He said that many of the people had interacted with these things before they became ill, and became "different" people. He said he was alarmed by the drastic personality changes in some of the people he studied. It was as if they were no longer present in their own bodies and some other entity was now in control. He spoke of people that were actually transformed into other strange identities. Their total personality changed, and sometimes even denied their true identity, claiming to be someone else. It was as if the original person was lost, now becoming someone else, therefore...crazy and institutionalized. A "Sally Smith," becomes "Jane Doe" and doesn't recognize her family, loses her memory, and talks of another life, as if she was never "Sally Smith" in the first place. No brain injury, no mental trauma, only the habit of toying with the occult. Many times this new "Jane Doe" personality was not psychotic or violent, just strange and disoriented. As if lost or trapped in a foreign world.

I was impressed by Tom's credentials and the realistic and logical method that he had used to arrive at his conclusion. It sounded as scientific as one could get on a subject that is not recognized as being science. I think he surely sensed my confusion, but after listening to Tom, I realized that there was logic based on the fact that, "When things consistently fail to compute, it does point to a consistently undefined possibility."

Although Tom appeared shy and a bit awkward in dealing with the subject, it was just his manner. Tom was still an active newspaper reporter, looking for a good story. Beyond doing research for a book, Tom was an avid student of psychic phenomena. He was well educated on the subject of ghosts, and a fair judge of legitimate true ghostly activity. In retrospect, he was an excellent reporter and investigator. He had us completely at ease and openly discussing all aspects of our experience. Within thirty minutes, it was as if we were dealing with an old friend.

We took Tom on a tour of the house. When it was finished, Tom informed us that the next step was that the building would be examined. He said that many times people like to play pranks by using electronics or devices to fool them, and though he felt this was not the case in our situation, it was a factor that must be eliminated. After spending three hours with us, he said he would return soon, bringing along a few other people who would inspect the building. We thanked him for his time and anxiously awaited the next phase.

Marsha and I were impressed. We both felt the fact that because no one came rushing in to see our ghosts, that these people may be more selective, and therefore more experienced at these things. We were also surprised that during the time Tom Valentine was visiting, the apartment was uncharacteristically quiet, with no activity whatsoever.

Tom Valentine had left us with hope. For the first time since our ghostly problem began, we felt that it could possibly be eliminated. We had only owned the building eleven months, but it truly felt as if we had been under this stress for much longer. It was hard to imagine that maybe, just maybe, our ghosts could be removed. It was hard to imagine that possibly this curse would no longer dominate our lives. It was hard to imagine that finally, we might get a decent night's sleep in our own home.

Although hopeful, I kept remembering Tom Valentine's comments. "Those who became other personalities and became lost or trapped in someone else's body," was a horrific thought. I kept thinking of people with no chemical imbalance, no brain damage and no trauma, just an interest in the occult, or playing with Tarot cards, séances, and Ouija boards, and remembering the Ouija board that we found in the closet. I wondered if old *Ben* had used it to conjure up the rest of his family before he died. I wondered if he had used it to talk with his suicidal dead wife. I wondered if crazy old *Myra* had ever played with it. She surely qualified for a mental institution. I did feel some comfort knowing that we had people involved that seemed to know of these things. Maybe soon this whole nightmare would be over.

"...we, the spectators, felt a strong gust of wind
that blew the curtains and rattled the blinds."

Carole Simpson, NBC Evening News.

Chapter Six

Exorcism

Tom Valentine called the very next day, on a Wednesday, and asked if Friday evening was open for a visit. He told Marsha that he was bringing along two people that would inspect our building. Marsha told him that it was fine, and that we were looking forward to the meeting. Friday came quickly.

It was already dark and about 6:30 P.M., when Tom's smiling face appeared at our front door. As promised, there were two people with him. My eyes fixed on Tom's companions. Strangely, my first impression was that they looked evil. With Tom, was a smaller man in height, who had jet black hair and a matching goatee. He had the serious appearance of someone prepared for confrontation, with thick black eye brows and piercing dark eyes, and a look that made it clear this was not a social visit. His name was Joseph DeLouise, a psychic. He brought with him another psychic, a female named *Barbara*. She too, had raven hair, dark eyes, and was dressed completely in black. My first impression was that I really didn't like the looks of these people, but I trusted that Tom knew what he was doing and was in control.

After being introduced, I couldn't help remembering the first group of so-called "psychics" and, indeed, these two seemed to fit in with that group...weird. Although friendly enough, they studied everything intensely.

There were no smiles, and their attitude was most solemn. When I initially shook hands with them both, I could tell that they were reading me, by the way they held my hand a few seconds longer than necessary. They did the same to Marsha. I scrutinized them closely, studying them as suspiciously as they were studying me.

We walked from the apartment entrance to the kitchen. For every step along the way, came a question. As we passed through the dining room, Joe asked, "Do you spend much time in this room?"

I answered, "No." He nodded, as if he already knew the answer.

As we walked past our bedroom doorway, he asked, "Is this is your bedroom?"

I answered, "Yes." Again, he nodded approval, as if he was telling me something I didn't know. I couldn't help but wonder, *'What kind of psychic is this?'* He sees that the dining room is barren and empty, and I could have guessed it was rarely used. Then he passes our bedroom, looking into a furnished room, where there are only two adults in the house, and asks if that's our room? Anyone might have guessed that also. As I led them to the kitchen, I was thinking that this was to be another wasted night. So far, I was being informed of what was blatantly obvious.

I imagine that they could easily observe by the expression on my face that I was not impressed. I couldn't help it; my face reflects my moods, so therefore I never play poker. As if to prove their ability, so that I might relax a bit, *Barbara* turned toward me, looking directly into my eyes, and said, "Bullets." The mere word struck me with complete surprise, also as amazing was the fact that I focused on the exact event and knew what she was referring to.

I said, "What?"

For some strange reason, I knew specifically what she was referring to, the moment I heard the word. But, I kept it to myself, as I decided to play this game through.

Again, she smiled and said, "Bullets." She observed my surprised--but smug--reaction.

Joseph DeLouise was smiling, as though he knew all along where this exchange was about to lead. Tom Valentine and Marsha were confused and observing. They had no idea what we were talking about.

I said to her, "What about the bullets?"

She smiled once again, knowingly, and softly stated, "Basement...bullets are in the basement."

Now Marsha was totally lost, as this whole exchange was making no sense, except that she recognized that I seemed to be playing some mind game that I was in control of...or so I thought.

I continued, "Where in the basement?"

Barbara smiled once again. "In a jar, in the rafters. There are bullets in a jar, sitting on a ceiling rafter of the basement."

This time, it was I that smiled. "You are correct. I found them there myself." I then explained to everyone that I had found a jar in the basement months ago and in that jar were some bullets. I carefully hid that jar on a beam or rafter, above the basement ceiling. No one knew about this except me. I had never even mentioned it to Marsha. I was completely amazed. I had almost forgotten about it, which made it even more amazing. I knew that *Barbara* sensed my skepticism and decided to use that event to relieve my doubts. Surprisingly, she chose the one thing that was relative to the building, but exclusive to my memory. There was no way she could have known that fact, or even guessed. I also knew that she couldn't have "read" my mind, for the bullet incident was buried far in the background and near forgotten.

In any event, from that moment, both Joe and *Barbara* had captured my full attention. I soon realized that psychics are not in total control of their power. It's not like a radio that can be turned on at will. It's a gift that they are given that sometimes controls them. Initially, I was guilty of assuming psychics should be able to know everything. This is a common misconception. A true psychic's power is normally intermittent, with many occurrences being unpredictable. Why she saw the bullets? Who truly knows? But she did. I anxiously awaited their next step.

They proceeded to ask us a long series of questions. It seemed Joe DeLouise had done his homework and reviewed the questionnaire that Tom had collected only a few days before. This time he wanted specific details about my job, our backgrounds, and about our existing relationship. I noticed that we were being asked the same questions in different ways, as if to bring out inconsistencies. I guess we passed the first test, as he moved on to other subjects. He was also very interested in our psychic ability.

Posing questions such as, "Have you ever had any dreams that came true?" or, "Do you ever rely on certain feelings, for no apparent reason? Such as driving to work and taking a different route, or avoiding someplace because you didn't feel comfortable going there?"

"Singing an old song, then, turning on the radio only to hear it playing?"

"Picking up the phone to dial someone who was already dialing you?"

Marsha and I both had many of such experiences, plus others, but always felt it was common and natural. Joe felt it may be otherwise. He said it seemed that we were both very strong, psychically. Our conversation eventually took a casual turn. Joe DeLouise was particularly interested in our cat's ability to sense the ghost's presence. We told him that Kitty did have the ability to see something, and it was something she didn't like. Her ordeal of being thrown or "lifted" through the window, twenty feet to the concrete, without a scratch, he found incredible. He was so impressed that he offered to buy her. Marsha refused, as Kitty was a wedding gift I had given her, and she loved her dearly.

Joe was fixated on Kitty, and found it very unusual that as he stared directly into her eyes, she stared right back and refused to look away. He was convinced that with her ability to see spirits, she may be a type of familiar.

They requested a complete tour of the apartment building, including the attic, garage, and yard. We agreed. Unlike the first group that covered the house in ten minutes, their tour took over an hour. From a distance, I watched as they traveled from room to room. They seemed to stop and "feel," or study, the exact correct places where we had experienced activity. We had previously unlocked all the doors and had given them the floor plans. They proceeded outside of our apartment on their own, only coming back to ask for a ladder, so they could enter the attic. We waited for them to complete their inspection.

When they returned, Joseph DeLouise and *Barbara* both appeared shaken. We all sat together in our kitchen. Joe was very serious when he looked to Marsha and me and said, "There is more than one ghost...and, I believe one of them is dangerous."

"Dangerous?" I asked.

"Yes, I believe one of them intends to do you harm." He stated.

"Ghosts can't hurt you...can they?" I asked.

"I must say this...yes, they can...they can do great harm, both physically and emotionally." He seemed sorry to say it.

"Are you telling me that ghosts can actually hurt you physically? Have you ever seen this happen?" I was completely astounded.

"Ed...I have had ghosts throw things at me. I have been hit many times by propelled objects." He said it so nonchalant that I felt ignorant for asking. I decided to play dumb about the background of the house, further testing their psychic ability. "So, tell me about our ghosts." I asked.

Joe started first. "I feel an old woman. She is here. She is harmless, but is imprisoned here for some reason. From her you have nothing to fear. But there are others. There are at least two men. One younger, one is much older. The younger one is evil. He must be removed. I believe it is this spirit that frightens me."

Joe was right on the money about the gender and ages of the possible spirits. I was impressed. *Barbara* then continued.

"There is one in the garage." She stated.

"In the garage?" This one was new to me.

"She hung herself." *Barbara* stated flatly.

It was at that moment that, for the first time, I gave away a bit of my knowledge.

"No, I was told that she hung herself in the basement." I blurted it out. "At least that's where the body was found and from where they removed it."

"No, she was definitely hung in the garage." *Barbara* spoke with authority. "If they removed the body from the basement, it must have been moved there, for she died in the garage."

I immediately thought of the bent garage key, a fact that they were totally unaware of. This surely would explain the bent key. I was a bit confused, for *Walter* did state that he actually saw the body removed from the basement. Marsha was dumbfounded, for she had no idea that I had captured so much knowledge about the history of the building. She was likely upset that I had also kept it to myself. Joe proceeded to talk strategy.

"I would like to do one more inspection of the building, without you and Marsha present. You see, both of you are very strong psychically. I need to know if one or both of you are drawing them out. I would like to return one more time with another minister, and go top to bottom again, except with the both of you gone. In fact, if you can arrange it with your tenants, I would like the whole building empty. Can you arrange that?" he asked.

It seemed a strange request, but I agreed. He said he would call and schedule it during the coming week. What started out as another evening of "wasted" time, in my estimation, turned out exactly the opposite. We had witnessed a convincing display of pure psychic ability. I cornered Tom Valentine and expressed my thanks, stating how much I was impressed. Tom told me that Joseph DeLouise was quite well known and that he had just written and published a book about him. When I inquired about the book, Tom went to his car, returning with a copy, and gave it to me. "Psychic Mission," it was called. Both Tom and Joe autographed my copy. I took a Polaroid photograph of them, both standing in my living room to use as my book mark.

We ended the evening with Joe giving us some personal readings. Marsha and I both were impressed by his ability to know things that were personal and private, or were past events unique to our lives. This little man with the strange goatee had a tremendous ability and power that was hard to imagine. I can still remember asking him if I would be financially successful. At the time, I was thinking of opening a hot dog stand as a side business. I tried to get Joe to specifically comment on my attempt at opening the hot dog stand. He carefully avoided being specific, as though he knew that my attempt in the food business would be dreadfully unsuccessful. I'm sure he did know, but stated emphatically that I would be very, very successful in my computer career. I didn't imagine that, for computers (at the time) were not in wide use and the programming profession was regarded as nothing more than a type of accounting clerk. I was overworked and underpaid. I thought he was definitely wrong. At that time, I did not see the explosion and advancement that technology would take, and I could never imagine my career becoming the nucleus of managing a business. Despite my doubts, he turned out to be quite correct, for years later I would find success as an executive in the computer software business. Fortunately, he did not inform me that a near fatal heart attack would actually force my retirement. Ignorance can truly be bliss.

Marsha and I felt that we were in good hands. Joe DeLouise certainly left us with the feeling that he was in control of our situation. He didn't mention how, but he had a plan of ridding our building of its ghostly inhabitants. We had confidence that our ordeal might soon be over. What we did not know, at this point, was that Joe knew these spirits would not leave easily--if at all. I would later learn that ghosts are not so easily removed. It is a fact that the vast majority can never be evicted. Only on rare occasion can a spirit be put to rest or driven out.

Joseph DeLouise grew up on the streets of Chicago. He was born in Italy, and Sicilian by birth. His manner of speech still remained spattered with "street" talk. He was once a professional hairdresser, before following his call into the spiritual world. Although Marsha and I had never heard of him, he was given national attention because of accurately predicting a number of high profile events. Like most psychics, he was plagued with visions of disasters, some of which had made him famous. However, it was a number of other future predictions that set him apart from the normal psychic community. Tom Valentine's book, Psychic Mission, becomes more interesting, and much more a testament to Joe's gifts, as decades pass.

Six months before Chappaquiddick, Joe saw the face of a drowning blonde woman, linking her death to the name Edward Kennedy. After being called in to assist on the Sharon Tate murder case, he quickly saw two men and offered descriptions matching Charles Manson and Charles "Tex" Watson. These and other specific visions propelled Joe into the national spotlight. But Marsha and I knew nothing of these events, only that we trusted the little man with the dark goatee.

It would only be a few days later that Joe would call us and schedule another appointment. He showed up on a Thursday evening. Along with Joe was an exorcist, Reverend William Derl-Davis. He was a tall, heavy man, with golden curls of long hair, and a deep, booming voice that had a precise English accent. Reverend Derl-Davis had a background of confronting spirits and demons. As he told us, he practiced such with the many haunted castles in England. Exorcising ghosts was common practice in England, so our situation did not disturb him in the least bit. With his thunderous voice,

I could easily imagine him commanding ghosts to leave. If not that, then I saw him playing "Hamlet" on the stage.

His commanding personality gave us confidence, but it was actually a false confidence. Being an exorcist, Reverend Derl-Davis was experienced in confronting demons, not ghosts. A demon can be confronted and driven out, a task he had accomplished many times. Ghosts, however, were a different story. It never occurred to me that although he had "practiced" in the castles of England, the castles still remain haunted, so his success rate with ghosts could not have been very good. In retrospect, Joe brought the exorcist into this because he feared that the one spirit was so malevolent, that it could possibly be a demon. This was a secret that they would not share with us immediately, and I was very glad that they kept it to themselves.

They had requested Marsha and me to leave for a few hours, along with our tenants. They wanted the whole building to themselves. We left without asking questions, deciding to take a drive and visit friends. We speculated on the reason for their private inspection; Marsha felt that they would try drawing out ghostly activity without us being there, as if to test the strength of our ghosts. I felt something totally different. Remembering how careful they were in their selection process, I felt that they were doing a more thorough inspection of the premises to guarantee that they were not being fooled by electronics or other tricks. We returned after a two hour period.

They were seated in our kitchen when we returned. I could see the ladder on the back porch and knew that they had been in the attic. They asked us to be seated. They appeared very serious and haggard, and possibly even worried. Joe said, "We indeed have a number of ghosts, and they should be removed." They stated that they would attempt an exorcism. In their expert opinion, they felt that it was possible to force them out. I was too hopeful to sense their lack of confidence at this point.

"What's an exorcism?" I asked. I had never heard the term before. *[I had not yet read the book given to me by my late Aunt Helen]*

Joe explained that it was a religious ceremony that was used to free earth bound spirits. He said he would also try to communicate with them by going into a trance. Once in a trance, he could hopefully convince them to leave. It was dangerous, he explained, but Reverend Derl-Davis would be present to help Joe maintain a certain level of his trance, for if he drifted too deep, a dominant spirit could expel him from his own body and take command, resulting in possession. I immediately had flash backs of my discussion with Tom Valentine about the mental institution where he had done research on people that had personality disorders. I remembered how he told of people that "became" other personalities. These were poor souls that had lost their complete original identities...so I began to understand Joe's fear.

Going into a trance, or attempting any out of body experience, is only inviting "possession," a word that is mostly associated with demons, not ghosts. But ghosts, too, can be looking for bodies to use, as I would soon learn. Joe DeLouise was taking a risk, and at the time, I couldn't truly appreciate the precarious position he was about to put himself into. He was going to make himself vulnerable to possession, in order to rid us of our ghostly problem.

Joe stated that the trance was the only way of possibly understanding exactly why they were staying here. He would attempt to remove that obstacle and "show" them that they were no longer of this dimension. He said he would ask God's assistance in bringing these spirits to peace. He urged us to put crucifixes in all the bedrooms, to protect us as we slept.

Reverend Derl-Davis was a nice enough individual, but Joe DeLouise was special. He was a people-person. He explained every detail of what he had encountered and how he would solve the problem. He sensed any insecurity or confusion, and offered advice and solutions before we could even ask. He counseled us on our future behavior, and cautioned us to avoid anything negative. It was these negative emotions that the spirits used to fuel their activity. Joe seemed to know that I had played with the ghosts, though no one had ever told him. He warned me not to do so, for it was very dangerous. I was not to call them out, nor address them any longer.

Having grown up in the inner-city of Chicago, I kept waiting for them to ask for something. Everybody wants something. Everyone has an angle, I thought. Growing up a Catholic, I was educated that even the Church wants something. A donation is expected for every service performed. Every family was given a registered set of envelopes, with which to submit their donations. This was so they could be totaled and measured each year. The

Pastor would let you know if your family wasn't properly donating. Our previous church even printed a list at year end, ranking the donations and printing them by family, from the most contributions to the least. It was always humiliating. It was natural that I sat there, waiting for the bill. It never came. Never did they remotely imply they expected anything. Needless to say, I was puzzled.

All Joe had requested was time to prepare, and said he would call us when he was ready to perform the exorcism. Marsha and I had hoped that this would finally bring our ordeal to an end. After a long, educational evening, they left, leaving us alone with our ghosts. It was as if the ghosts knew we would attempt to evict them, for they became more active than ever. That night, as we went to bed, we could hear the arguing echoing from the back porch. We knew, that they knew.

The next day, while I was at work, Marsha and *Ellen* sat together, talking and passing time. Marsha told *Ellen* about the exorcism and how the ghosts would soon be gone. *Ellen* held hope that the process would succeed, for then they wouldn't have to move. If the ghosts were really gone, she felt *Dave* would reconsider moving out.

Marsha immediately changed her habits, as Joe had suggested. When the phone lifted off the hook, instead of getting angry, she casually replaced it, controlling her emotion. As if testing her emotional strength, the ghosts became much more active in the kitchen area. Her hand mixer would not stay put on the wall. But instead of getting upset, Marsha laid it on the counter and ignored it.

When the flickering kitchen lights became a distraction, she merely shut them off, showing no emotion. Marsha would use every bit of her will power to heed Joe's advice. We both understood that they were taking their best shot...or so we thought.

It was a few days since Joe's last visit when the phone finally rang. Marsha hoped it was Joe, scheduling the exorcism. Instead, it was NBC News Correspondent, Carole Simpson. She was calling personally, requesting our permission to cover and report on the exorcism. That night, Marsha was excited when she told me of the call. She asked what I thought about it. I didn't see a problem with allowing NBC to film it, providing it would be a serious work. My only fear was that they would use us as "entertainment," for amusement purposes. I did not want them making a joke of our misery, or making fun of us on national television. Being a professional computer programmer, I did not want to be portrayed as a "kook." This could definitely hurt my career, as my craft was dealing in logic. Marsha said that Carole Simpson had sounded sincere in stating that it would be a serious piece. Ms. Simpson said that she would like to interview us first, and we could make our decision at that time. We agreed we would go that far and schedule the interview. It was our assumption that NBC news had found out about the story from Tom Valentine, having been an ex-journalist.

Actually NBC had learned of our house and situation from a Father Joe Wood, who had a radio program on NBC. Joseph DeLouise had called Father Wood about our predicament, for advice. Likely, it was Father Wood that informed the news department.

The interview took place the following evening. We were both familiar with Carole Simpson, having seen her many times on our local news. She was a very prominent local journalist. It was actually exciting, having her sitting in our living room. She appeared more of a business woman than the classic image of the frazzled reporter. Initially, we just talked pleasantly about our experiences. She made no attempt to take notes, though she had a note pad at her side at all times.

We were both very surprised that unlike a "probing reporter," Carole was asking us questions about our ghosts, that were always accompanied by a question concerning the emotional aspect of living with such a problem. She almost seemed more interested in us, than she was with the actual haunting. We literally talked for hours. We found Carole Simpson entirely different than what we expected, and were honored that she was to do this report personally. She was a very warm, caring, professional person. Years later, it would be almost predicable that she would be promoted from local news to a top Washington correspondent and national news anchor. She was a very intelligent, professional lady, with a touch of class. She was very experienced at putting us at ease.

Over the course of a few hours, we related our story. I was candid in telling her that my fear was that we would be ridiculed as being insane or imagining things. I did not want to be made fun of or labeled as a kook. She promised me that if NBC did the story, it would be done as a serious piece, in a professional manner. We believed and trusted her, and she, indeed, kept her word.

She said that NBC had never before covered an exorcism, and that it was possible that this piece would make more than just the local news. She anticipated many hours of filming. First, a film crew would film footage of the house, inside and out, possibly at different times of the day, to catch different moods, due to lighting. Then, she would film an extensive formal interview with Marsha and me. Finally, they would be here to film the exorcism, and a post exorcism interview. She explained every aspect of what we would experience. When done, we felt comfortable and positive about letting NBC do the coverage.

At the end of the meeting, she left us a list of phone numbers where she could be reached, at any time. She asked to schedule the film crew for the next day, stating that she would be there to check on them. We agreed with her plan. During this whole process, I kept expecting the "boom" to fall, with Carole changing to the typical, cynical, sarcastic, probing reporter. One who would find our exorcism questionable and possibly even with the focus of humor. It never happened. She spent three days and many hours on this project, and remained the same warm, sincere human being, on camera and off.

The next day, bright and early, the NBC film crew arrived. They filmed everything. For the better part of six hours, they continued their work. I couldn't believe how much footage was collected to do this piece. I watched as these creative people began moving cameras throughout the building, taking footage at weird angles and varying lighting conditions. I was anxious to view the final product, given the resource and effort used. When the complete house had been filmed, the stage was set for Carole's interview with Marsha and me. It would be done in our living room.

These were days long before our sophisticated technology. This film crew traveled with literally a truck load of huge lights and cameras.

Unlike what I had imagined, it was a casual interview. Yes, there was special lighting and cameras, but no director yelling "Take one!" and "Take two!" Carole merely sat opposite of us and proceeded to ask us questions. Within minutes, Marsha and I were no longer conscious of the fact that we were being filmed. It was like old friends having a pleasant conversation.

Never did they stop tape, or want us to do specific things or say anything scripted. It lasted about forty five minutes and was completely painless!

Carole never played the devil's advocate by questioning our sanity or religious convictions. Never did she smirk at the mentioning of the word "ghost", nor did she ever stage us to look foolish. Being a professional, she could have easily done so and we never would have known it until we saw the final cut. When all was said and done, Marsha and I were pleased with the experience. We both felt that we were able to tell our story in a serious, meaningful way.

As they packed up, we were told that they would return the day of the exorcism. As of that moment, it hadn't been scheduled. We were all left waiting for the next step.

It was that very evening that we received a call from the office of Joseph DeLouise, scheduling the exorcism for that coming Friday. We were warned that it could take from two to six hours. We were also asked to have the children removed from the building during that time. Marsha and I had no idea of what to expect. Marsha still had the book, "The Exorcist," given to her by my departed Aunt Helen, but neither of us had read it. This was possibly a blessing, for had we read it, we probably would have been very, very frightened.

* * * *

Strangely, the night before the exorcism, the building was silent. For the first time in a very long time, you could hear a pin drop. There seemed to be no activity in the building. The doors remained closed, there were no voices or footsteps in the hall, and the kitchen lights never flickered. Kitty seemed to travel from room to room without a hiss. It was almost as if our ghosts anticipated what was about to take place, and were storing up their energy.

It was at about 9 A.M. on a Friday when the NBC News van pulled up to the building. There was also another car filled with people accompanying them, plus Carole Simpson in her own car. Altogether, there were eight NBC people. They proceeded to unload their equipment, carrying it up to our second floor apartment. One could feel the electricity in the air. I soon realized that only three people were necessary for this "shoot," and that the rest were merely curious and here to simply observe an exorcism. The word of our paranormal activity had gotten around, and it was my assumption that a few NBC management types wanted to see what a "real" haunted house looked like.

While they were setting up, I could hear the comments. "What if we see a ghost?" one of them asked. "I'll be out of here so fast...you won't see me move..." said another. They were teasing each other, as if they were visiting some kind of carnival.

Carole Simpson was sitting with Marsha on the couch talking as I watched the technicians do their thing. I noticed that the sound technician was the only person not joking. I knew why, without ever asking. His face had the same expression that I had seen so many times on my tenant, *Dave*. The sound tech was obviously frightened. I walked over to him and asked whether it would be okay for me to set up my own tape recorder. He replied, "No problem," as his wide eyes darted about. I could tell he was on the edge, and I knew that if I snuck up on him and screamed, "BOO," he would have probably jumped right out the second-floor window. It seemed that he was the only one having a serious problem.

The equipment was all in place and tested when Joseph DeLouise and William Derl-Davis entered. Davis was wearing his clerical robes, as was Joseph DeLouise. It wasn't until that moment that I realized that he, too, was an ordained minister. They carried a large leather case. At the sight of the ministers, the NBC crew became silent. As Reverend Derl-Davis moved the dining room table into the center of the room, he asked, "May we set up here?" On the table, he set his leather case.

First, he pulled out a fine linen table cloth and covered the table. Next, there came two candle holders, in which he placed long, tapered white candles. Then, he produced a large brass crucifix on a stand, and finally, a large bible. When finished, the dining room table resembled an altar. Joseph DeLouise was not his usual cordial self. He sat quietly off to the side of the room, and I believe he was praying in silence. The festive excitement was replaced by quiet anticipation. Then, William Derl-Davis spoke. As he did, the sound tech, who was wearing headphones, flinched at the sound of his thunderous and commanding voice.

"Do all of you intend to stay during this ceremony?" he asked.

One by one, everyone nodded 'yes'. Then, he threw a curve.

"Everyone must realize that once we begin, no one may leave this house until the ceremony is concluded." By the sound of his booming tone, we knew he wasn't kidding and that he would make no exceptions.

Everyone started looking at each other, as eyes darted around the room. Instantly, there was a conference of some of the NBC people. I overheard, "No way. No way am I going to be locked up here if all hell breaks loose...I'm leaving." Quickly, three of the NBC people left, only bidding a fast farewell. Then, a fourth said, "Goodbye," exiting down the front stairway. Then, two of the remaining NBC people began having an emotional discussion. One of them was the sound tech. In the middle of the discussion, William Derl-Davis threw them another curve.

Looking back, I took personal satisfaction at watching these NBC suits, who acted so juvenile, scurry out like scared little children.

"I strongly urge anyone staying to wear a crucifix."

This caused more stress. It now became evident that the sound tech wanted to leave. This became a problem, because he was the only sound technician in the group. The NBC group now held another meeting. We watched as a heated discussion took place. Carole Simpson, though concerned, played no part in it. We gave her a large cross to wear during the ceremony. Finally, one of the NBC men approached me. He said that the sound man would stay, but only if we gave him a cross to wear...and a bible to sit on. I quickly provided both. With that, the sound tech stayed and the other man left. Carole Simpson was left with one camera man and one sound man. The other five men were gone. When things settled down, Derl-Davis presented the agenda.

"We will begin by praying for God's assistance. At the appropriate time, Minister DeLouise will go into a trance, attempting to make contact with the spirits in this house. You might notice him waving his hand in air. For your information, in his hand is a small cross and mirror. He will attempt to have the spirit approach the cross, and when doing so, they will also face the mirror, which will display no reflection. With this, hopefully they will realize that they have no reflection and are no longer of this world." He took a deep breath and continued.

"I must ask you for complete silence. You see, when Minister DeLouise is in this trance-like state, it is very dangerous. I will be observing him closely, attempting to keep him from drifting too deep into his trance. We can never be precisely sure what will happen in these situations, but try not to be alarmed and remain silent...and no one leaves this building until we are completely finished."

Though he had a commanding stage voice like James Earl Jones, I knew William Derl-Davis was not acting. By the expression on his face, it was clear he was stepping into the unknown and in fact, he appeared troubled. As they both knelt by the table and prayed in silence, beads of perspiration appeared on their faces. We all watched in a hush, only glancing to each other, as if asking, "Are you okay?" The one person I knew who was not okay, was the sound tech. As he sat next to his recorder, pointing the boom mike in the direction of the minister's, his eyes were bigger than the gigantic headphones he was wearing.

We watched from the adjacent living room as they prayed. After about twenty minutes of prayer, Minister Derl-Davis asked, "Are you ready?" Joseph DeLouise nodded and arose. Derl-Davis then positioned two chairs facing each other.

As William Derl-Davis watched intensely, Joseph DeLouise fell into what appeared to be a very relaxed state. His eyes closed and his breathing became very deep. As I watched, I could see him wince, as if in pain. It was about that moment that everyone felt a strong gust of wind. So strong, it rattled the blinds. The crashing of metal blinds almost blew the headphones off the sound tech's head. Everyone felt a tinge of fear, because we all knew that there were no windows open. You see, the sound technician had previously made a big deal about having all the windows closed, so he could control extraneous noise. All of us were thinking the same thing; where did the gust of wind come from? I noticed that everyone was doing the same thing I was doing--clinging to the crosses that we had hanging around our necks.

We could feel a change in the immediate atmosphere. The air became thick and heavy. The room became dark, as if the sun had disappeared. We could all feel the room temperature drop noticeably. Everyone became aware that something was taking place. We all felt the presence of something unknown.

Joseph DeLouise then uttered, "You must leave. You don't belong here." His arm shot out and he displayed the cross with the small mirror attached at the top. He was holding his arm to his right...but we could see nothing.

Again, he stated, "You do not belong here. You must leave." Then, as if explaining, "Can't you see that you have no place here? Why do you stay?" he asked.

Everyone leaned forward, as if we expected an answer to materialize out of thin air.

Reverend Derl-Davis then said, "Come back, Joseph...don't go too far. Come back...come back."

Joe then took a deep breath and spoke, except this time his voice was different; so different, that it didn't sound like his voice. "The picture...the picture...I need the number." It sounded exactly like a woman's voice; like a weak, old woman's voice.

Derl-Davis seemed stunned, as though this was not anticipated. "Why does it concern you?" boomed Minister Derl-Davis. "Why does it concern you?" he asked again.

All who were in the room realized that he was addressing someone other than Joe DeLouise. But it was DeLouise that spoke this strange voice. "I need the number," the voice stated.

"You are not of this world. Look at the cross. You no longer belong here." As he spoke, he perspired freely. Joe's face became twisted, as if in pain. Derl-Davis then commanded, "Come back, Joseph...come back. Don't go any further. Come back!" He was visibly concerned, and we became witness to a brief interval where it appeared that things might be out of control. Joe didn't respond, and his face was very contorted.

"Come back, Joseph...come back." Derl-Davis beckoned.

Again, the strange voice spoke. "The combination...the number...I need the number."

"Why does it concern you? You do not need the number any longer." Derl-Davis responded.

Then in his own voice, Joe spoke as he held out the cross and the mirror. "Look, you cannot see your reflection. You must leave this place, as you don't belong here."

All of us shared the same expression of concern. It appeared the spirit had taken over Joe's body for a brief instant. The sound of that voice gave everyone a bad case of the chills. It was the sound tech that picked up on the next strange occurrence. I could see him flinch, followed by him immediately adjusting his dials on the machine. He was hearing something that only he, initially, could hear. He was hearing a single bird...chirping. The chirp of the bird seemed to pierce all other sounds.

Soon, we could all hear it. The single bird soon multiplied, as the sounds began to accumulate and amplify. Then, there gathered more and more birds, making the sound that was impossible to filter out. There was only one tree outside in the immediate vicinity, and without looking, we all knew that for some strange reason, hundreds of birds were gathering. We listened, as the background sounds escalated and eventually became part of the recorded piece. As the trance-like confrontation continued, the birds seemed to continue to multiply, as the sound was fuller and louder. Later, when I played it back on my tape recorder, it was unbelievable. You could hear first one, then two, continuing until it sounded like a thousand birds. It must have been a nightmare for the NBC sound technician, who was trying to filter it out--and failed, as it was heard clearly on the news coverage.

Joe's trance continued, as he was trying to convince the ghost to leave. "You must leave this place," he demanded, holding out the cross with the mirror. We watched in awe. Although Joe DeLouise seemed to be in control, Reverend Derl-Davis looked very concerned. He kept repeating, "Come back, Joseph; come back."

We all knew that something was happening, but all of us were confused as to what. It seemed this continued for about an hour, with Joe demanding the spirit to leave, and Derl-Davis beckoning Joe not to go too far. Suddenly, as if waking up, Joe relaxed and opened his eyes. We could all see that he was completely drained of energy. Derl-Davis asked, "Are you finished?" Joe just nodded, slowly.

I did notice that Joe was not smiling. He didn't appear victorious. He certainly didn't look satisfied. I assumed that he was just drained of energy. Derl-Davis sat with him for about ten minutes before standing and facing the make-shift altar. He prayed in silence. Then, turning to face us, his voice rose to make an announcement.

"This house is clean. This house is pure. Anything that bothers

the individual in this house, comes from the individual himself." His expression was not convincing, as he bowed his head and continued.

He asked, "If you would all remain here while we seal the house with blessed salt." He helped Joe to his feet and they proceeded to spread salt across every opening in the building. Every door and window, from the basement to the attic, was sealed. I watched from a distance as they climbed the rickety ladder on the back porch to the roof. They didn't miss a single opening. It was about thirty minutes before they were finished and had joined us. Again, I noticed that both did not appear satisfied or successful. Their mood was serious, if not bothered. My assumption was that they were just plain tired.

Although both ministers spoke of a successful exorcism, their body language and expressions stated otherwise. I noticed how they seemed depressed. After a short interview, they soon left us. It seemed neither wanted any part of additional news coverage. I felt a great debt to them for what they did--or attempted to do. It was all done out of the goodness of their hearts, as they never asked for anything...not a dime...nor a donation. I could tell by the post interview that neither had any previous contact with NBC News, leaving me wondering how NBC even became aware of this.

Carole Simpson spent a long time sitting with us and just chatting. It was as if she forgot that she had an interview to finish. Finally, she remembered, and we finished filming. Much like the first interview, it was casual conversation with no uncomfortable or embarrassing questions. When it was all done, we thanked her for being so nice. Later in life, I would meet media personalities that weren't so nice, but Marsha and I will always remember Carole Simpson as a class act. Her final comment was that she would call us to let us know when the segment would air and to follow up on how things are going.

When everyone was gone, Marsha and I sat in pleasant silence. We never voiced a doubt. In our hearts, we wanted to believe that this ritual had ended our distress. We drove to my mother's house to pick up our daughter. When we returned to the apartment, we checked in with *Ellen* on the first floor, to see if she had heard any noise in our apartment while we were gone. She happily stated, "It was silent." This was good sign. We spent the evening watching television and reliving the day's events. The house remained silent.

I moved my tape recorder into the bedroom, where we, again, listened to the sounds of the exorcism and the various pre and post discussions. Listening to the pure sound, the gathering of birds was more pronounced. There were also other sharp loud sounds that we couldn't identify and didn't remember hearing at the time.

A "tapping" or "knocking" sound could be heard, clearly. Neither Marsha nor I had been aware of this sound during the ceremony. The most alarming sound that I had captured was the sound of a child. We could hear it call, as if far, far away, "Momma?" We played it...and replayed it. Since the exorcism had been done during school hours, no children were in the vicinity. But even if they were, we were two stories up, with the windows closed. It seemed we captured a sound from beyond.

Eventually, we went to bed that night with a peace of mind that we hadn't had for about a year. We agreed that something spiritual did take place, and felt that our ordeal could very well be over. As I drifted off to sleep, the words of William Derl-Davis echoed in my mind. **"This house is now clean. This house is now pure. Whatever bothers the individual in this house, comes from the individual himself."**

I awoke at 5 A.M., opening my eyes and facing the clock. I had my back to Marsha. I could clearly hear the sound of a woman crying out in great anguish. She was crying and sobbing uncontrollably. The sound was coming directly from our living room! I first reached behind me, assuring myself that Marsha was there. I was frozen in place. The familiar goose bumps set in, as I couldn't believe my ears. I was facing the open bedroom door, and could see that no one was in the living room.

I whispered, "Marsha...are you awake."

Since I didn't move a muscle and had my back to her, I only heard a quite, "Yes."

I then whispered, "Can you hear that?"

She answered, "Yeah."

Marsha whispered in my ear, "What the hell is it?"

I responded, "I have no idea, but it's coming from the living room. I can see there is nothing there."

"What are we going to do?" She questioned.

As I rose slowly, I whispered, "I'm going to record it."

I moved to tape recorder, which was still plugged in. I was almost at the bedroom door, and was only 12 to 15 feet from where the sound originated. It was dead center in the living room. The sobbing was loud and uncontrollable. It was the worst sound of anguish that I had ever heard in my life, and have ever heard since. The instant I flipped the record switch, it ceased in mid-sob. The house was, once again, silent. Whatever it was, it didn't want to be recorded. I had never, ever heard anything like that in my entire life. It was so unearthly, that I would remember it exactly as it was, for as long as I live.

Marsha ran to the front bedroom, checking on Christine, who was still sleeping soundly. "Eddie, I'm scared," was all she could say.

I thought for a second, then replied honestly, "I hope she was crying because she's leaving...if not...I'm frightened, too."

Looking back, I realize that the collaboration of Joe DeLouise and William Derl-Davis was likely the first and last time they would work together. It was a classic mismatch. DeLouise, a psychic, had no fear of going into a trance and communicating with spirits. Derl-Davis, being an exorcist, on the other hand, had a total fear of any out-of-body experience. He saw it as an open invitation to a demonic procession. When DeLouise went into his trance-like state, Derl-Davis was sweating profusely and always repeating, "Come back," for fear that something uninvited might enter. I guess it was a clash of two very different philosophies. DeLouise wanted to communicate and solve whatever problem this earthbound spirit had, while Derl-Davis only wished to expel whatever manifested.

"Ghosts are not demons. It is a mistake to think that
They can be exorcised."

Edwin F. Becker, 2011.

Chapter Seven

Surrender and Retreat

Within the week after the exorcism, it was evident that it was a total failure. Marsha and I felt guilty, as if it were our fault. It may sound ridiculous, but we actually blamed ourselves. The words of Rev. Derl-Davis reinforced this feeling.

"This house is clean. This house is pure. Whatever bothers the individual within these walls, comes from the individual himself."

Could this be our fault? Was it us that was drawing them out? These were the questions echoing in our minds. Nothing had changed. In fact, it seemed like they had more energy than ever before. There was no explanation for the sound of the woman crying in anguish; a sound we would never ever forget. Thankfully, it never happened again.

It was no surprise that *Dave* and *Ellen* would leave, as the activity in the first floor apartment resumed as if no exorcism had ever taken place. They quickly found another apartment, giving us notice that they were moving. They had been with us for about seven months. Likely, it would be seven months that they would not soon forget. Marsha was sad to lose her daytime companion, and was apprehensive of, once again, being alone in the building all day.

We received a follow up call from Carole Simpson. She seemed so concerned that we felt there was no value in having her worry about us. So we lied and told her everything was quiet and peaceful. She was very glad to hear that, and congratulated us and said she would call when our story was scheduled to air. We also received a call from Joseph DeLouise. He was concerned about us and whether we were having any problems. He specifically wanted to know about any additional problems, as though he knew the exorcism had failed. At least, that was my suspicion at the time. Knowing I was dealing with a psychic, I didn't lie, but did say everything was going okay. I believe Joe sensed the problem, for he maintained an almost weekly contact with us for quite some time.

Regarding Carole Simpson; as time passed, I was always amazed that she has been overlooked as far as being a pioneer in television history. This woman, who walked with Martin Luther King and anchored national news, shattered many barriers. She became a premier reporter in Chicago, then was recruited to a national news desk in Washington, all at time before Barbara Walters was a name and when Oprah was still in school. Carole seems to have been ignored by journalism history. As we watched her career progress, we felt honored to have known her. All women in journalism owe her a debt.

After *Dave* and *Ellen* moved out, I went about the task of cleaning the first floor apartment, preparing for the next tenants. It was during this work that I saw the "old woman" that I was so familiar with for the last time. It was late on a Sunday afternoon when I was in the first floor apartment, cleaning. I was in the kitchen on my hands and knees, scrubbing the floor. The apartment was completely empty. As I scrubbed in front of the door that led to dining room and living room, I felt that someone was there. You know the feeling; as if someone is watching you? I glanced up and saw her. There was the old woman that I had seen so many times on my front steps. This time, she sat in the empty front room in her wheelchair.

I watched as she looked toward me, and then turned her head and glanced out the window. I studied her, and she appeared as solid as you and I. Again, she went through the same motion, looking toward me, then out the front window, as if attempting to tell me something. Though she appeared solid, her image was hazy, as if my eyes were blurred. In the blink of an eye, she was gone. For a moment, I was frozen in place, for there was no doubt that I just seen a ghost.

I walked slowly to window, exactly where she had sat, and looked out.

There stood her son, standing directly in front of building and just staring. I recognized him, for he lived down the block. He was an old man, just standing there in his old woolen coat. He appeared defeated by life, with his hunched over appearance. He had a sad expression on his face. I wondered if he felt sorry for walking by the apartment all those years, ignoring his mother, who had been sitting at this very window, calling his name. Year after year she sat, trying to get his attention as he walked by, ignoring her. I wondered if he mourned the loss of any chance of reconciliation.

I also wondered what it was that would cause that type of situation, where a son disowns his own mother. When he saw me look out at him, he slowly walked on. Strangely, I was not frightened; in fact, I felt that I understood why her exorcism could never have worked. To this day, I believe that the only thing that could have released her spirit, was the reconciliation with her son. Because I never saw her again, I would like to believe that's exactly what happened that Sunday, in spirit. Maybe, just maybe, he came there to make his peace and released her.

I never mentioned this whole experience to Marsha until much later. That evening, when I was finished cleaning the first floor, my sister called. She said she really wanted to move into the apartment. I tried my best to discourage her, but *April* would not accept a negative answer. She demanded to move in. I tried explaining that I didn't like taking rent from my sister, but she stated that either way she would have to pay someone, so why not me? In the end, she convinced me and would move in the following month.

It was during this time that Carole Simpson called to inform us that the story would run on NBC news, both in the evening and late night news. I asked a friend to tape the segment on an industrial video recorder. It was actually an early form of video tape used for security systems. This was long before commercial video VHS machines. This recorder used only black and white tape, a half inch wide. Although I had this tape, I never played it, as I never had a machine that was compatible. Years later, NBC gave me permission to convert and duplicate it for whatever my needs.

Only recently with current technology were we able to view this piece, frame by frame, and realized that in one camera shot that was supposed to be of the empty dining room, was an image captured. In the doorway, a small white object is seen moving where no one is present. Since we were all behind the camera when this shot was filmed, the movement and object is unexplainable. Our ghost actually made a short, undiscovered appearance on this film!

The night the segment ran, we gathered around the television. It was much better than I had expected. Although introduced with a smile by NBC's Jim Ruddle, it was almost documentary quality. Surprisingly, it was rather long, running 5 minutes and 11 seconds, at a time when the total local news was a thirty minute program. We watched it at six o'clock, and again at ten. We were pleased with what we saw. The next day, Carole Simpson called to ask how we liked it. We told her we were pleased, as it was treated seriously. She told us that after running the segment, NBC received a record number of phone calls. Carole described the NBC switchboard lighting up like a Christmas tree. Consequently, the segment was to run again during the week, both at six and ten, and also on the weekend edition of their network news.

Carole stated that they had so much usable footage, that it might be considered for an extended segment on NBC's new program, "First Tuesday." This was a "60 Minutes," type program, similar to today's "Dateline" or "48 Hours." We would later learn that it did run on "First Tuesday." Unfortunately, it did not run in Illinois, because the segment had aired so many times on network news. We never saw the extended segment, but other family members in California stated that they did.

Shortly after the news coverage aired, our phone was ringing off the hook with various reporters asking for our story. We did agree to be interviewed by one reporter. He claimed he had been given approval by Joseph DeLouise and NBC to do the story. I believed we owed Joseph something for his efforts, so we agreed to be interviewed. It wasn't until after we granted the interview that we found out the reporter actually represented a tabloid paper, The National Tattler. The Tattler was a direct competition of the National Enquirer. In the Tattler issue of January 16, 1972, a full page story appeared. Although the basic story was correct, the reporter embellished it with many inaccurate details, attempting to sensationalize it. I was sorry we granted the interview and was embarrassed by the errors it contained. As it turned out, Joe DeLouise had never asked for any article to be written, and the whole incident was a result of creative negotiating, on the part of the reporter.

Joseph DeLouise called to mention that his phone was also ringing day and night and asked me for a favor. He asked if I would appear with him on a radio program, the Jack Eigen Show. He said he would like me to tell the story myself. I had no desire to be on radio, but seeing that Joe had never asked for anything, I agreed. I knew nothing of radio, and had never heard of Jack Eigen. My mistake. I should have done my research, for Jack Eigen was famous as one of the cornerstones of early talk radio. He also had a personality that made Don Rickles seem like a pussy cat. Eigen was well known for interrogating his guests and playing Devil's advocate.

I met Joe at his apartment and we had plenty of time to talk. I learned a lot about this man, who was given a gift that could also be called a burden. He had no control of when his visions might take place. Sometimes, they were identifiable, and at other times, vague, leaving him to guess at the time or exact location of an event. Many times, he saw his premonitions in the form of newspaper headlines that were sensationalized, yet limited and abbreviated. On occasion, he could get distinct impressions by the touch of a person or their belongings. Given our discussion, I believe he learned that ghosts, unlike demons, could not be exorcised. I had the distinct impression that ours was his first and last attempt at an exorcism.

His apartment was in a trendy area, near downtown, and was not what I had imagined. It was tastefully furnished in modern furniture and decorated in soothing earth tones. I guess I expected all types of psychic paraphernalia to be scattered about, and instead, found it void of anything but simple décor. I'm not sure exactly what his impressions of me were, but my impression of Joe was of a lonely man, very burdened by his calling. The main impression I had, was of a man who seemed dedicated--if not obsessed--with helping people.

Eventually we proceeded to the radio station. Mr. Eigen seemed nice enough before the program began, but when the "On the Air" sign was turned on, his personality changed. I knew by the way he introduced us as guests that we were the Christians, and he was the Lion. He was the epitome of all my fears. It seemed it was a non-stop slew of absurd questions and skepticism. Joe was the main target, enduring a verbal onslaught of abuse. Eventually, Eigen asked my story and I told it in capsulated fashion, giving Joe the credit he was due. While I spoke, Eigen sat silently, to my surprise, for I expected him to start shooting barbs. When I finished, he simply asked, "Do you drink, Mr. Becker?" It was a cynical tone. The people in the studio laughed, and if looks could kill, Eigen would have fallen over and he knew it.

He returned to brutalizing Joe DeLouise, as Joe was more passive and made a perfect target. I knew Eigen was avoiding me, for he saw something in my eyes. It was the fact that he knew I might explode and the three second radio delay may not save him. I was upset by this obvious set-up to bring a few laughs to his show at our expense. I was allowed to tell a bit more of our story, and for Joe's sake, I lied and said everything was fine and our troubles were over. What purpose would be accomplished by saying otherwise? Our segment was rather long, as Jack asked opinions of everyone on the program. A master of radio, Eigen then made fun of us by making humorous comments at the others on the program that believed our story. He had about ran out of ridicule when he asked Joe to pick horses at the racetrack. As a psychic, Joe was conditioned to this type of treatment, and I was not. To this day, I will never understand how these gifted people endure this type of treatment from the media. I truly felt sorry for Joe. I felt that if I were a psychic, I would surely keep it to myself, rather than endure this type of media exposure. Joe thanked me for coming with him, and apologized for how it turned out. Since the show aired at midnight, I felt that nobody I knew was listening anyway. I taped the show on my reel to reel, but never listened to the tape. I still have the tape, and am saving it for a day when I really want to raise my blood pressure. Joe and I kept in touch for a few years, but the last time I had contact with Joe DeLouise was the year 1995. Informed of this manuscript, he had intentions of writing the Foreword.

As years passed, I did realize Mr. Jack Eigen was a master showman. Actually, he did nothing more than give the audience what they expected. He was a legend in talk radio, long before talk radio was popular in prime time. Unlike today, Jack Eigen could entertain without having to use foul language or gutter humor. He also had integrity about most of the products he advertized, and as I learned, he frequented the restaurants and used many of the products he promoted. We should be so lucky as to have a show like his today! God Bless him.

We did have a final visit from Rev. William Derl-Davis. He, too, was concerned for our welfare. He seemed guilty and sad, and seemed to know that the exorcism was a complete failure. He explained the difference between a spirit and a demon. Dealing with a demon that will expose itself and confront an exorcist, was his forte. He admitted his failure in dealing with spirits, and told us stories of many castles in England. He explained the many kinds of spirits, with most being benign and harmless. It seems each spirit has its own unique reason for being earthbound. This reason must be addressed before a spirit can be put to rest. Ghosts cannot generally be driven out. This is what he felt about our ghosts, except for one, which he warned was definitely malevolent. Our ghosts had a strong bond to what they still believed was "their" house, with at least one being possibly dangerous. He advised us to wear and display as many blessed items as we possibly could. He left us with his own bottle of holy water. What he implied, in his own way, was for us to move out. We never saw Reverend Derl-Davis again, and learned of his mysterious death only a few years later.

My opinion was that at first visit, Joseph DeLouise sensed our malevolent ghost and collaborated with Reverend William Derl-Davis because of the possibility it might be a demon. I believe that the night they asked us to leave our building, they attempted and failed to exorcise that spirit. I believe that going into the taping by NBC, that they both already knew that failure was eminent. In socializing with Joseph DeLouise, I believe the one thing he withheld was the advice for us to move. Maybe in being psychic, he already knew that we would survive. At least, that is what I like to believe.

* * * *

There was no doubt that we had no option that would allow us to move. All we could do was try to never address the spirits, and to accumulate blessed items, which we would display about the house. No sooner than *Dave* and *Ellen* were out, my sister began bothering me to move in. After much reluctance, I eventually agreed.

My sister was excited about moving in. On that day, it was like a huge family party. We were approaching Christmas, and the family spirit combined with the season made it a happy event. Her sons, my two nephews, were five and two years old. Her husband, *Jim*, was a very easy going guy. They had a nice family. In one weekend they were settled in, as if they had lived there a year. My sister made a point of showing me her new piano. It was an old upright, with ornate carvings. She was proud of it, and had a right to be, as it was beautiful and sounded as good as it looked.

Marsha and I were candid about the existing ghostly activity, and the fact that the exorcism was a failure. I warned my sister not to fuel the situation, but she was anxious to witness an event. It would not be long before she realized that she, too, could have the chandelier move simply by walking in the dining room and looking up. As the weeks passed, *April* became more and more excited as the ghosts revealed their personalities. She became so obsessed with the activity, that she would make a mistake that I believed would change her whole life. She bought a Ouija board.

I would not be around to stop her, for I soon came up with a solution for Marsha and me. It was shortly after the failure of the exorcism, that I found a way out. I would get a second job, in order to get the money to buy another building. I took a job doing programming evenings, from six to ten at night. I calculated that it would only take about six to eight months before I could start shopping for another property with a low down payment, or at least have enough for a security deposit to rent another apartment. Marsha didn't like the idea of spending more time alone in the apartment, but I explained to her that it was our only way out. Fortunately, Marsha had my sister to keep her company--or so I thought.

I was engrossed in working and saving every dime I could. My weekday routine had me up at 5 A.M., working my day job from 7 A.M. until 5 P.M., bringing a sandwich to eat in the car between 5 P.M. and 6 P.M. in the evening, and then, working until 10 P.M. and getting home for in bed by 11 P.M. Saturday, I was up at 5 A. M., and was off work early at 1 P.M. I became a robot, with only one thought--to get out of this trap. During which time, I was totally unaware of what was going on in my sister's apartment.

April was twenty-one years old. She had told all her friends about the ghosts in her apartment. Because of the media exposure, everyone wanted to see the authentic haunted house. Still within the Age of Aquarius, there was no shortage of young flower-children types, wanting to communicate with the dead. *April* soon took to having candle lit gatherings, creating a séance-type atmosphere. It was a few months after she had moved in when we talked and she had told me how the ghost was playing her piano. She actually sounded happy about it.

Much like I had done with *Ben* and the kitchen door, *April* called out *Ben*, to play a few keys. Only it wasn't *Ben* that was playing. I had no idea of the extent of her involvement, but I warned her that it wasn't funny and to leave *Ben* alone. I told her to buy a cross, have it blessed, and wear it. I had bought crucifixes for every room in our apartment, and suggested that she do the same.

April continued toying with the unknown. There was no shortage of friends that wanted to see her piano play a few keys on its own. They would sit in a candle lit living room and concentrate on calling the spirits. All the common events would occur. The basement door would open, the chandelier would swing, and lo and behold, a few piano keys would play. My sister became very popular. Her apartment became a gathering place for dozens of people that wanted to experience a new "awareness." Then, came the Ouija board.

Apparently, she had been using the Ouija board for some time before Marsha became aware of it and told me. *April* had invited Marsha downstairs to witness what was happening. Marsha entered the candle lit session, with *April* and a few friends working the board. They were asking it questions, and getting answers. *April* was very cognizant of the fact that her piano playing spirit was not *Ben*; she knew it was a spirit named *Henry*, because the board told her so. Marsha watched as the pointer moved from letter to letter. When *April* asked, "Why are you here?" The board spelled out, "NO."

When *April* asked, "When will you leave?" The board again spelled out, "No."

Marsha was frightened, as she was as much aware of the danger, as I. She, too, had heard the story of research done by Tom Valentine. She watched, and although three people had their finger tips on the pointer, it moved freely when responding to questions. Marsha knew that *April* was playing with dynamite. That night, when I came home, she spoke of the séance and the Ouija board. I was in a trance created by overwork. I answered her, "Yeah...yeah," but I never really heard her, for I was only looking forward to my four or five meager hours of sleep.

It was a few weeks before I became aware of changes in my sister. It was a Sunday evening when I heard my nephews' screaming. I walked down the stairs to their back porch and could hear my sister yelling at her husband to beat them, because they were being bad. I had never seen her in this type of rage before. I knocked on the door and when *Jim* opened it, he was holding a belt. I walked in, and *Jim* appeared embarrassed. I looked to my nephews, who were crying and trying to catch their breath.

I asked, "What the hell is going on?"

Jim put his head down and stood silently. My sister was still very much upset.

"I told *Jim* that they deserved a good beating. He can't even do that right! Those kids should get what's coming to them. All day long they aggravated me. All I want is for *Jim* to be a father and do his duty." She was in a terrible state.

"*April*...enough. They've had enough." I stared her down.

"Oh that *Jim*, he can't do anything right, Can you, asshole?" She glared at him.

Jim just stood there with his head down. Blonde haired and blue eyed, he was a big man of about six foot and 180 pounds. But at that moment, he looked like a lost little boy, unaware of what exactly was happening. He looked as confused as I felt. I had never seen my sister act this way, nor for her to argue or criticize her husband in public. *Jim* assured me that the incident was over, but I left very worried over what I had witnessed. I explained to Marsha what I had seen. Marsha said she had definitely noticed that *April* had been changing. Marsha suspected it was the Ouija board. The word hit me like a sledge hammer.

"Ouija board?" I uttered in disbelief.

"Yeah, I told you about it weeks ago." Marsha was perplexed.

"You did? When?"

"Eddie, I sat with you when you came home and told you about the Ouija board. It scared me."

"Jesus Christ, I was probably half asleep. *April* has been playing with a Ouija board? How long?" I was in shock.

"For a long time. She has her friends over and they use it. They burn candles and talk with the spirits. I saw the damned thing move!"

"What exactly did you see?" I asked.

"Well, *April* would ask it questions, and the pointer would move, spelling answers. She called him *Henry*."

I near fell out of my chair. I knew about *Henry*, but had never shared it with anyone once old *Walter* had told me. If *April* was addressing him as *Henry*, it was certainly *Henry* that she was talking to. Everything that Tom Valentine had told me about people playing with the occult flashed through my head.

"That's it, I'm going downstairs."

I went down the back stairs and banged on the door. My sister answered.

"Where's the Ouija board?"

"Why?" *April* responded.

"I want it and I want it now." She knew that I meant business. Without saying another word, she produced the board, handing it to me. Once I had my hands on it, I smashed it to pieces. *April* never said a word to stop me. I told her never, ever bring a Ouija board into the building again. I marched back up to my apartment, and it would be a week before *April* and I would talk again. When we did, I knew she was in big trouble.

It was the following Sunday when she stopped up to see me. We all sat in the kitchen. It was almost out of the blue that she turned the conversation to the ghosts.

"Ed, I think you're possessed." It was as if she was stating a casual fact.

"Why the hell would you say something like that?" I asked.

"Well, when you smashed that Ouija board, I never saw you get that angry before. It was as if someone was controlling you."

"*April*, I really wasn't that angry. I was as concerned as I was upset." I was telling her the truth, for I was more concerned for her well being.

"I saw a face behind you, when you were talking." She stated.

"Whose face? What did it look like?"

"It was a disturbed face. He had brown hair. It was alongside yours, slightly shorter than you." *April* was describing *Henry*.

"*April*, I don't think I'm possessed, but I do think that you are in trouble. You should move out." I responded.

"Are you kicking me out?" She asked.

"No. I'm not kicking you out; I'm telling you that you should leave before something happens." I have always felt guilty about my response, for I should have evicted her, if necessary, in order to save her from pending terror. I knew she had seen *Henry*. I also knew that it was likely she had conjured him up using the Ouija board. I had a strong feeling she would be seeing him again.

She rose to leave. "I just wanted to tell you of my suspicion that you might be possessed."

I had an open shirt on and held up my cross. "See this? If I were you, I'd get one...for the whole family." As I responded she left.

I turned to Marsha. "Am I possessed? Do I act like I'm possessed?" I needed confirmation that I was okay.

Marsha smiled, "I don't think so. Obsessed, maybe. Compulsive, always. But possessed...No."

Her words made me feel much better, but I was worried sick about my sister. I decided to corner her husband, *Jim*, on the next opportunity, to find out how things were really going.

* *

It would only be a few days before *Jim* and I ran into each other while taking out the garbage. Once in the yard, I asked him about my sister.

"*Jim*, Is my sister having problems?" I asked.

He smirked, as if I touched a nerve.

"Yeah, she is, and I don't understand it. Lately, she is always on edge. It's like she is always mad about something. And the kids...Jesus Christ, there are times I think she's going to kill them." He was clearly worried.

We both lit cigarettes, standing in the alley way. *Jim* took a long drag. "I blame her friend, you know. Lately, they come over and burn candles, talking about the unknown, ghosts, Edgar Cayce...whatever. I'm sure glad you broke that Ouija board; that ritual was getting real crazy." He took another long drag of his cigarette. "Maybe it is the kids, being locked there all day with them. Maybe I should encourage her to get a job. What do you think?"

I swallowed hard and blurted it out. "*Jim*, I think you should move. I think that the ghosts are getting to her. I'm not kicking you out. I'm only saying this, because I have watched her change also. She seems obsessed with communicating with them and to drawing them out. I truly believe it's dangerous for her."

"Nah, I don't think it's that. It's not any ghosts." He shook his head.

"Well, have you heard the piano?" I asked.

"Yeah." He answered.

"You've seen the chandelier sway?" I asked.

"Yeah, many times." He answered.

"The door? The footsteps? The arguing?" I asked.

"Yeah, yeah, yeah. But I still don't think it's the ghosts. I think it's being locked up with the kids, combined with all her crazy friends."

"*Jim*, I'm going to be honest with you. I'm working my ass off at two jobs, in order to get the hell out of here. I never believed in ghosts, but I do now, and feel like something bad is going to happen if we stay here. It's not like the place is going to blow up or anything, but like we're all going to be crazy after a while, just like the family that lived here before us. They were all off their rockers. If I can't save enough to buy another place, I'll rent another place in order to get out...I'm serious. I feel sick that I let you guys move in." I emptied my soul.

"Ed, this has nothing to do with you. It's *April*. She's just going through some changes." *Jim* really wanted to believe that. "See you." He crushed his cigarette and headed toward the house.

I felt sick to my stomach. Although *Jim* and I couldn't agree on the source of her problems, it was clear that she had plenty of them. I felt sorry for *Jim*, for I could see the confusion and worry on his face. They had married young when my sister became pregnant, at seventeen. They had enjoyed growing up together. Now, it was evident that they were growing apart. My sister had a great temper. Being 5'8", she would almost stand eye to eye with *Jim*. Her hazel eyes would burn red with her German heritage. It wasn't long before *Jim's* Irish and *April's* German would create arguments that would silence the ghosts.

April was confiding in Marsha that she was having nightmares. Always bothered, she felt as though she was being watched. She complained that she constantly felt something brushing up against her. More than one time, a hand was felt on her shoulder. *April* started to believe that *Henry* was after her, and that he was bothering her day and night. While I worked, Marsha slowly watched my sister deteriorate.

* * * *

I had been working two jobs for five months. Reading the classified section at lunch, I came across an interesting ad. *'Desperate Seller needs Buyer. Two Flat building, near Montrose and Ashland. Phone 555-5555.'* Why I called that particular ad, I'll never know. But I did. It was a local Real Estate agent. *Hans* was a friendly man with a strong German accent. He told me of a family that had sold a building which was located much closer to my job. They used all their cash to purchase another building in Wisconsin. The problem, was that the sale fell through. Now they were stuck with two mortgages. Since they had a lot of equity, they would sell for any reasonable offer. We agreed to meet the next day at lunch, as that was the only free time I had.

The next day, my first question was how little of a down payment could I get by with, even before I knew the asking price. *Hans* stated 20%, because if the buyer accepted a low offer, they wanted a guaranteed sale. Only with 20% down would a guaranteed conventional mortgage be approved. I told *Hans* that this was impossible, and thanked him for his time. *Hans* must have sensed my desperation, for he asked if I would consider taking out a loan.

I told him it was out of the question, because it was illegal to borrow your down payment during these times. *Hans* said it could be done, if I wanted it bad enough. He now had my full attention. *Hans* had a buddy that was a vice president of home improvement loans at a local bank. He said it could be fixed so I could get the loan as a home improvement loan... cash up front.

I was puzzled, as I knew there was little equity in the Campbell Street building. If they appraised the building and compared it to my mortgage and what I owed, I wouldn't qualify for more than a $500 loan. *Hans* said not to worry. He showed me the listing for his building. It was at $24,000 dollars, which was much more than I could afford. He said if I offered 18,000 dollars, they would accept, if I had the 20%--or $3600 dollars. He guaranteed I would easily get the loan from his friend's bank, for there would be no appraisal, because the "fix" would be in.

I quickly took a pencil and paper to the numbers. I would own two buildings with two apartments each. I would live in one and rent three. I added up the expected rents, then, compared that number to the mortgage payments, plus, the home improvement loan payment. Bingo! It made sense...I could easily do it. The three rents would cover both mortgage payments and my personal cost would only be the payment on the "home improvement" loan.

I told *Hans* "Let's go for it." I was so anxious, that I could have almost signed the contract before I even saw the building. We scheduled a visit to the building on the coming Saturday afternoon. I was very excited, but still skeptical of getting approval on this "home improvement" loan to be used as my down payment. If that could really happen...it would be a miracle. I wouldn't tell Marsha until it was done.

Saturday, immediately after work, I met *Hans* at the Ashland Street building. It was a breath of fresh air. The building was immaculate. As I walked from room to room, there was nothing but good vibes. It felt like a home. A wonderful Italian family owned it and had occupied both apartments. They were carpenters by trade, and had their own business. I guessed that they were good at their craft, for the building boasted of ornate woodwork and fancy cabinets. The head of the family retired and bought a huge house. He was taking his whole family with him to Wisconsin, where they would reestablish the business. They enjoyed talking, and I enjoyed listening. I asked just enough questions to learn the most important fact-- nobody had ever died in this building, to their knowledge.

Hans and I proceeded to his office. He explained the timing. First, I would go to the bank on Monday, applying for the $3600 dollar "home improvement" loan. That could take up to 30 days for approval. We would not submit a contract offer for a week or so. He felt that with the time to think and worry, the sellers would likely accept my first offer. All I needed was $500 dollars down, initially, to accompany the contract. We wrote up the contract, and I gave him my check. This was the second building I had purchased without telling my wife. I would wait until I had the loan approved and the contract accepted, before building up her hopes. Until then, I would go about my business of working sixteen hours a day, as usual.

* * * *

Marsha was becoming more and more frightened. The activity in our apartment was the same. But my sister, who was a constant visitor, was having major problems. *April* complained to Marsha of her nightmares. She said she always dreamed the same dream. In it, she was visited by a dark, hooded figure. She started to believe she was going to die. She was also hearing voices. She stated that whenever she was at her sink and washing dishes, she heard a voice telling her to kill herself.

The piano that was so entertaining, became the source of terror to *April*. Certain keys would play in the wee hours of the morning. It was always the same keys, the same volume, and the exact same number of times. Four notes, played over and over and over.

April was worried about her oldest son. He was talking to someone that wasn't there, on a regular basis. Her son called him *Henry*. If *April* spanked him or punished him, her son would threaten to tell *Henry*. *April* told Marsha that it was *Henry* that was touching her and playing the keys on her piano. *April*'s whole personality had changed. She was no longer happy, as that feeling had been replaced with fear and paranoia. She became almost manic. Talking a mile a minute, chain smoking, moving or pacing at all times, her thoughts became dark and negative.

Jim, her husband, didn't help the situation. Though he observed the activity and would awaken in the night at the sound of the piano playing, he maintained his denial at the mention of ghosts. Consequently, he was working so hard at denial, that he had no time to recognize what was happening to his wife. If he did recognize it, his denial would not allow him to attribute it to the ghosts. Therefore, he would take no action.

* * * *

Hans was correct. The "home improvement" loan was approved. Never was my Campbell Street building appraised. It was my assumption that a private deal was made between *Hans* and his banking buddy. If there was, I certainly wasn't involved and couldn't have cared less. I went to the bank and picked up my check for $3600 dollars, quickly depositing the money in my savings account. The Italian family had accepted my offer on their building, and now I actually had the down payment to buy it. It was a done deal, and was time to tell my wife. Marsha and I would both have to apply for the new mortgage. Though my approvals came during the week, I would wait for Saturday to tell Marsha. I would take the day off of work and we could visit the bank together. I didn't say a word about it for the balance of the week. It was Saturday morning when I gave her a clue.

Marsha woke me up at 5 A.M., as normal.

"The hell with work, I'm not going in today. Let me sleep another hour... okay?" I rolled over. I was sure she was shocked, for this had never happened before. Typically, if I had a heart beat, I went to work. An hour later, I arose for my morning coffee.

"We need to go to the bank together this morning. I need you to go with me." I said it as if it was just a routine matter.

"Oh Eddie, do I really need to go with you?" Marsha didn't really want to pack up the baby and go through all the preparation for a mere routine stop at the bank.

"Yeah, you have to be there. You see, we're applying for a new mortgage." I offered no more information.

"New mortgage? We have a mortgage. Why do we need another mortgage?" She queried.

I smiled as I drew out my answer. I knew it was the answer that she could only dream of. "Because...I bought another building! A few months from now, we're out of here!"

I thought Marsha was about to faint. She collapsed to a chair and immediately lit a cigarette. "How soon can we leave?" That was the only thought on her mind. She didn't ask what I had bought, nor where it was located. She only looked forward to leaving ASAP.

I explained the deal I had made and how it was a conventional mortgage. Instead of the five to six month approval we had experienced with the FHA, this would be approved within 90 days. So today was a big day. First, it was off to the bank and the mortgage application, then, a visit to our new apartment building. Marsha was on her feet getting ready in a flash. I intended to make a day of it. As a treat, we would eat out and spend the balance of the day visiting.

April and Jim, had invited my mother and brother over to spend the weekend. No sooner than Marsha and I had left, the activity in our apartment began. My brother would later describe the sounds of people walking around upstairs, as if we were home. They were fooled more than once that day into coming upstairs, expecting us to be there. But it was not until late that night did it get truly frightening.

We finished our day by stopping at my friend George's. There, we would stay at his house until about midnight. Back at Campbell Street, it was about 11 P.M. at night, when a loud crash was heard overhead in our empty apartment. My brother, Butch, said it sounded similar to an explosion. They had just gone to bed on the first floor. It was silent and dark when they heard a loud boom. Butch described a sound that vibrated the entire two-story building. Everyone was alarmed and arose, turning on lights. The crash centered in the front of the building, in our living room area, and the sound traveled from the front to the back of our apartment. My sister ordered her husband to go upstairs and see what happened. Butch and Jim ran up the front stairs to find that we were not home. They then went back down stairs and up the back stairs, in order to look in the kitchen window.

The apartment was dark, with nothing to be seen. Marsha and I entered the back porch at about 1 A.M., to find everyone waiting up for us. My brother-in-law and brother followed us up the stairs, for they "knew" something was wrong. To their surprise, everything was fine, with nothing out of place. Butch and Jim went back downstairs to bed. It was about 3 A.M. when Butch awoke to sound of piano keys playing. He described it as if someone was plunking the keyboard. A single note would play. Not until the sound was through reverberating, would another note play. It was the first time Butch had ever heard this. It continued for about 15 minutes. It was all he could take. My brother said it was the last time he would ever stay at the Campbell Street building. He would refuse to return.

* * * *

'My sister was coming unglued,' is how Marsha described it to me. April was plagued by nightmares, and claimed she was being touched by someone.

She claimed to see the ghost of a male figure regularly. Her son was always talking to *Henry*. She complained that she couldn't escape him, day or night. *April* had abandoned her interest in Ouija boards and séances, no longer wanting any part of encouraging the paranormal. But it was too late. I believe she had opened a door to the unknown that she couldn't close.

Since our new building would be completely vacant, Marsha offered *April* to move in with us. Marsha wanted the first floor apartment, and *April* and *Jim* could live on the second floor. After discussing it with her husband, he decided the Campbell Street building was more convenient to his job. *April*, who was so excited about living there, was now depressed about having to stay. Marsha tried to convince *April* to wear a crucifix and to display a crucifix in her bedroom, but the advice fell on deaf ears. *April* felt that this would not help.

* * * *

I told *George* that we would soon be moving. Of course, he offered his strong back immediately and I accepted. Our new apartment had a finished basement, so, including the first floor, it had much more living space. I mentioned to *George* that there were a few things in the Campbell Street basement that I no longer needed. One of which was a portable work bench. *George* knew that his father wanted one, and offered to buy it. Instead, I gave it to him. He asked if he could pick it up the following Saturday morning. Since I would be at work, I stated that I would leave the basement door unlocked.

The following Saturday at about 9 A.M., *George*, and his sister, *Arlene*, pulled up to the Campbell Street building in his Cadillac. The work bench would fit easily in the huge trunk. They proceeded to the basement, via the rear outside entrance. Upon entering, *Arlene* could see the work bench toward the front of the basement. She guided *George* to the bench, where she would carry the front, and he would follow, carrying the rear. The table was light, but bulky. As they walked toward the exit, the sound of running water broke the silence. *George*, in his blindness, was puzzled. "What's that?" he asked.

What *George* couldn't see, was *Arlene*, frozen in place; the old laundry sink was the source of the running water.

"*Arlene...*" *George* said, "What the hell is that?" He could feel that she had set her end of the table down.

"The faucet on the sink...it just turned on by itself!" *Arlene* stated in disbelief. She watched as the hot water gushed at full force into the old concrete sink, with steam now rising.

"It turned on by itself?" *George* asked.

"Yeah." She answered.

"Who is down here?" *George* asked.

"No one at all. Just you and I." his sister replied.

"Aw, bullshit. There has to be someone here." *George* just couldn't believe it.

"*George*, there is no one here. Just you and I...I swear." As *Arlene* responded, and as suddenly as the water had came on...it stopped.

"Who turned it off?" *George* asked.

"It went off by itself. Let's get the hell out of here, *George*." *Arlene* was scared.

"Okay, but lead me to that sink before we leave." *George* was curious.

She led him to the sink, where *George* felt and examined the faucet. It was an old, brass lever-handle faucet. It had one handle for hot, the other for cold. He turned it on and off, realizing it was not easy to move, as it was very old plumbing. Now it was he that wanted to leave, and leave quickly. They carried the bench out the back door and to the car, where they loaded it into the trunk. It would be years later that *George* would confide that he was afraid to give the work bench to his father. He would confess that he and *Arlene* unloaded it into his garage, and gave it away the very next day. He didn't want that bench in his house. All the while maintaining that he still didn't believe in ghosts!

* * * *

The ghosts seemed furious with us. I believe, to this day, that they knew we were about to move and that they were taking their last shot. It was the Sunday after we applied for the mortgage that Marsha and I went, visiting relatives and spreading the good news of our future move. That afternoon, we returned to the apartment. It was a half hour before Marsha noticed that Kitty was gone. Again, we started searching and calling frantically. I went to our bedroom, where I found the window opened, about 12 inches. I knew instantly what to expect. Without even looking out, I ran out the back door and down the stairs. There, I found Kitty, cowering on the concrete, two stories below the open bedroom window. This time, when I picked her up, her nose was slightly bloodied.

I examined her closely. Other than a trace of blood on her right nostril, there wasn't a scratch. I was puzzled. I knew she couldn't have hurt her nose in the fall, for it was only a scratch and an insignificant one, at that. I was completely amazed. Had Kitty truly fallen from over twenty feet, she would have been hurt badly. I was worried that maybe this is where this phenomena would wind up. Maybe next time, they would drop her the whole distance. I carried her to the apartment. Marsha was hysterical. It took us a few minutes of discussion to realize that neither of us had opened the bedroom window. We both knew who did, however. I promptly got my hammer and nailed it shut. I believe it was at that point, that I took the upper hand in our ghostly relationship.

I watched Marsha crying and holding Kitty, and was sick inside. I became more and more angry. I wanted a confrontation, and wanted it badly. Over the months of our ownership, gradually I understood the ghostly possession. I finally understood that it was their house. They had built it, owned it, and died in it. We were mere guests. They could entertain us or harass us at their whim. It was that Sunday that I dealt them a crushing blow. I started to have thoughts of burning the place down! I promised them that if anything happened to hurt my family or my pets again, I would torch the place. Insurance began to look appealing!

I felt that I had nothing to lose. I truly believe that this was the factor that caused them not to escalate further activity in our apartment. I meant every word of my threat. I knew exactly what I was thinking and at the time, it made perfect sense. They had screwed up my whole life, turning it into a nightmare. My wife was a nervous wreck, my pets were terrorized, and I had lost two dogs. My family and friends were scared to death of visiting. My sister was losing her mind and I was working day and night. Enough was enough. I wanted revenge. I would strike back by destroying the one thing they needed most...the building. I started having specific thoughts on how I would go about burning it down. Yes; I was starting to lose it. I wondered how they would like living in a vacant lot. I knew, that they knew, exactly what I was thinking, and that this was no bluff. They had pushed me too far.

I believe that they could sense my hatred and intense anger. I also believe that they knew it was focused on the one thing that they feared. There was no faking it; it was hatred and revenge rising up from within me. All I ever wanted was a place for my family to live. All I ever did was put all of my effort and time into rehabilitating "their" property. I had hit my limits. I began wondering how they would feel, wandering about in a pile of rubble!

"Ouija boards provide some classic examples of dealing with Earthbound entities who have no regard for the living."

Joseph DeLouise, Psychic Mission, 1970.

Chapter Eight

Relinquish At All Costs

As we counted down the days, the apartment was normal, in its own ghostly way. The kitchen door still opened, the phone continued to lift off the receiver, and the mixer would still float to the floor. But, knowing we would soon be moving made everything easier to cope with. Our loan had been approved and the closing date was set for October 1st.

It was when the leaves were beginning to turn and the nights became cool, that I decided to start the gas space heaters for the winter season. One evening, I attempted to light the pilot on one of the two gas space heaters. I turned the dial to the start position, lit a match, and pushed the pilot button. No luck. The pilot wouldn't light after many attempts, so I gave up on that heater and moved to next one. Going through the same routine in trying to light the pilot, it produced the same result. Neither heater would start. It was as if the gas valves were turned off again. I knew it wasn't the main valve, because our gas stove and dryer were working fine.

I remembered that the separate gas valves for the heaters were in the attic. I grabbed a flashlight and headed for the back porch. Climbing a ladder and squeezing through the trap door in the roof, I faced the window entrance to the attic. I opened the window and entered. I hated going up there at night, though I wasn't sure why. I couldn't enter the attic without getting a chill. I ignored it as I shined the light, looking for the valves. After finding the first one, my suspicion was correct--it was turned off. Looking for the second one, I was hesitant, for I had to move deep into the attic, as it was way in the front of the house. I eventually found it, and it, too, had been turned off. As I turned to leave, the window entrance to the attic slammed shut. Although it gave me a chilling feeling, '*It's just the wind,*' I thought. I proceeded downstairs for my second attempt at lighting the space heaters. This time, I was successful.

The apartment was soon warm. Puzzled by the gas valves being turned off once again, I did not attribute it to ghostly activity. But then again, given my thoughts of arson, maybe the ghosts became slightly paranoid of flames? I just knew that I certainly did not touch them.

The next morning, I awoke to a cold apartment. Initially, I wasn't sure if the heaters were off, or Marsha had turned them down. Going for my morning coffee, I learned the heaters were, indeed, off, as Marsha had never touched them. Curiously, I attempted to light one pilot, unsuccessfully. It was if the gas had been turned off yet again--yet the stove worked fine, so I knew it wasn't so. Having to be at work, I would deal with it upon returning later that night.

Tired from a long day, it was another trip to the attic with my flashlight. I really disliked going up there. Up the ladder, through the trap door, and squeezing through the window entrance, I found the same thing as I had found the previous night--that the valves were turned off. For a second time, I turned them on. They were just simple lever gas valves; turn the lever one way and it's on, the other and it's off. But they were very tight and not easy to turn. Returning downstairs, I lit the heater once more. I knew who had turned them off. You could only reach the attic with a ladder from our back porch, and no one had done so since the first time I had turned them on. Now, I became angry and upset.

My first thought was that my ghosts might turn the gas off, and then turn it back on, leaking gas into the apartment. Checking the heaters, I found that if this was done, only the pilot light would leak, which was of no harm. I felt better knowing they were not trying to "gas" us out. This event never happened again. I eventually came to the conclusion that given my thoughts of burning the place down, maybe there was some connection and they really had lost their fondness for flames.

My sister, *April*, continued to spend her days in our apartment, keeping Marsha company. Her life had become a nightmare. Although our ghostly activity had been put in check, hers was escalating. She complained that she was afraid to sleep, because of the nightmares. The piano that she had loved so much, was about to be put up for sale, because of the playing that went on in the middle of the night. She could no longer stand hearing the single notes echoing.

April insisted she was being touched. "He puts his hand on my shoulder," she would complain. Marsha watched as my sister was deteriorating before her very eyes. She had lost interest in her children, and started treating them as if they were a punishment that she had to endure. Her relationship with *Jim* became one of resentment and hostility. She had lost weight, was pale, and had bags under her eyes from not sleeping. She would jump at the slightest sound. She would talk to herself openly, while also conducting conversations with other people.

I approached her husband a second time on the subject of moving with us to our new apartment building. He refused. Campbell Street was closer to his job. What was happening to *April*, he had written off as changes she was going through. *Jim* would not say the word "ghosts." Therefore, he refused to attribute her problems to the proper source. I gave it my best shot and could do nothing more. My sister and her family would stay in the building.

Moving day couldn't come soon enough. Every time we moved, Marsha always had a list of items that she wanted for our new apartment...but not this time. She didn't care about curtains, drapes, carpet, or anything else. She just wanted out. She actually started packing a month before closing day, and made me promise that we would be out that same day--and that is exactly what happened. On October 1, 1972, we moved.

Our new building had a warm feeling. It truly felt like a home, even before we unpacked. Again, *George* had come to the rescue. It was in the wee hours of the morning when we loaded the rental truck. The closing was set for 11 A.M., at which time we had to be at the bank. So we hustled and were loading before the sun came up.

This time, our closing went smooth. Unlike the Campbell Street closing, there was only one family and one attorney to deal with. It was completed in less than an hour. We drove right from the bank, in our rental truck, to our new home. George and I lugged all the furniture and boxes while Marsha unpacked. That first night in our new building was the most restful night that Marsha and I had spent in almost two years. Though we still owned it, the Campbell Street building seemed a world away. We went about the business of renting our old apartment.

I advertised the apartment at a very attractive rental price. I was looking for someone who would maintain the whole building in exchange for the bargain rent. It wasn't that I didn't want to maintain it; it was that I wanted to avoid going there for any reason. Ray and Lynn filled the bill.

They were a young couple with two children. He drove a garbage truck and did side work at various construction jobs. She was a housewife and homemaker. He agreed to take care of the building. Mowing the grass, painting, simple plumbing or repairs, all became his responsibility, provided I pay for the necessary material. It seemed we had found a solution that would remove any need for us to visit Campbell Street.

Lynn was a tall, statuesque blonde, with blue eyes. Ray was dark haired and muscular, with a smile that reminded one of a young Paul Newman. There was never any mention of ghosts. Marsha and I had mixed feelings about disclosing the potential problem, but it was I that insisted we keep it a secret. I felt that if we told potential tenants about the ghosts, we wouldn't get anyone to rent the apartment. I also felt that if they didn't antagonize the ghosts--as I did--the activity would be minimal and maybe even ignored. At least, that's what I wanted to believe.

Everything was going our way. We had our new home, our apartments were completely rented, and our lives settled into a normal existence--but it wouldn't last. Only a month after moving out, I received a phone call from my brother-in-law. My sister had disappeared.

He went on to explain that the previous night, April couldn't sleep. She sat up by herself, smoking and listening to the radio in the kitchen. When he awoke, she was gone. Other than her purse, she took nothing. Calling the police, he found that a person would not be considered missing for at least 48 hours. He said that he had called everyone he could think of, with no result. She had totally disappeared.

I was in shock and didn't know what to say. Jim assured me he would call if he heard anything. Marsha and I could only speculate as to what would cause *April* to abandon her family and walk into the night, without money, clothes, or anything else. Though it was a surprise, we had both expected something of the sort would eventually happen. *April* had welcomed the ghosts and communicated with them. She had played with the Ouija board. *Henry* was a normal sight to *April*, both in her conscious state and in her dreams. She was consumed by ghosts that had hounded her day and night, and obviously, she could take no more.

We both knew that there had to be an event that caused her to flee the apartment in the wee hours of the morning. We wondered what exactly happened that was so frightening that she would abandon her belongings and family. We never found out. Even to this day, *April* will not discuss exactly what took place that night, and sleeps with the light and radio on, 40 years later!

The next day, *April* called from Cicero, a near suburb of Chicago. She was not coming back to Campbell Street, she told *Jim*. She didn't care about anything and said she would not go back under any circumstances. She was leaving her husband, children, and all her belongings. What the exact dialogue was between *April* and *Jim*, I will never know. However, the end result was that *April* was gone, and *Jim* now wanted to move out. He was moving in with his mother, who would watch the kids so he could continue working. It would be years before I would see my sister again. To this day, I live with the guilt of allowing her to move into the Campbell Street apartment. I will always believe that this caused changes in her life that she was never able to recover from.

I had no problem renting once *Jim* had moved. I merely placed the ad, and had *Ray* and *Lynn*, our "caretakers," interview prospective tenants. By the beginning of the following month, we had new tenants on the first floor of Campbell Street. But problems would continue and there seemed no escape.

Our tenants' would mail us the rent check on the first of each month, but three months into their stay they called and asked to deliver it personally. One evening, they stopped by to deliver the rent. We invited them in for coffee and cake. After settling the rent, we enjoyed casual conversation. But, eventually the conversation took a familiar twist. It was *Lynn* that brought up the subject.

"Did you ever have anything unusual happen in that apartment?" She asked.

I knew what she would say, before she uttered the words. I watched as she blushed, as if she were embarrassed to bring it up. She also looked to her husband, as if beckoning him to add to the subject.

I gave Marsha the "don't you dare open up" look, and responded. I played dumb.

"Unusual? Like what?" I asked innocently.

"Well...like...noises, or things moving." She was struggling to describe something that she hoped we would catch on and add to. But, we didn't.

"Noises? Things moving? Like what?"

She paused, and I could tell at that moment, *Lynn* was not sure whether to continue...but she did.

"My broom moves by itself." As she spoke the words, she stared at us with her big blue innocent eyes, hoping that she didn't sound completely crazy. *Ray* was looking down at the floor, as if embarrassed, and she continued.

"My dishes...they...break. They fall off the shelves. Did you have any problems while you were there?" She pleaded.

I knew that Marsha would not let *Lynn* suffer by allowing her to continue describing her problem any longer. I looked to her in a manner that told her it was okay to talk about it.

"Yes. We did have a few things happen." Marsha stated. "I had a mixer that wouldn't stay on the wall and also had a phone that wouldn't stay on the receiver."

I watched as the weight of the world came off of their shoulders. They breathed a sigh of relief that we clearly understood.

"Then there is a ghost?" *Lynn* asked.

"We think there might be." I answered.

Ray now entered the conversation. "Whew...I thought we were going completely nuts."

"No, an old man died there, just before we moved in. In fact, that is why the building was originally for sale." I offered.

"Are you frightened?" I asked.

"No, no...no." *Ray* responded. "I thought we were going crazy. Our broom moves itself, right out of the closet into the kitchen. We couldn't believe it! Did it move your broom?" He asked.

"No. We never had a problem with our broom, only the mixer and the telephone. Nothing scary, mind you, just aggravating sometimes." I looked to Marsha as I spoke, letting her know not to offer any more than what we already had.

"Six dishes." *Lynn* blurted. "Six dishes have been broken so far. I have had pots and pans move...but only a couple of times."

"We had the apartment blessed when we moved in, but it didn't do any good. He never really bothered us, but we knew he was there from time to time." I told her.

"He? Are you sure that it is a he?" *Lynn* asked.

"Well, we assume it's a he, because that is who died in the apartment." At this point, I couldn't tell whether they were amused or bothered by the ghost. "He never really bothered us; we ignored him most of the time. Have you had a problem keeping the kitchen door closed? Like maybe, it opens by itself?" I probed.

Ray answered. "Yeah. It opens now and then by itself. It doesn't bother us much. We just wanted to know whether we were imagining things and if this was even possible."

We continued discussing the ghost, and though I held my breath, expecting them to give us notice, it never came. They left that evening satisfied that they could account for the mysterious events they had experienced. I knew that this was just the beginning, and that we would hear from them again. But it was not *Ray* and *Lynn* that I would hear from next; it was my new first floor tenants, the *Scotts*. Mrs. *Scott* called me, less than a month after moving in. We had never met, but she was given my phone number for emergency purposes. She introduced herself, and sounded like a very nice lady.

"I wonder if you could help me?" She asked.

"Sure. What can I do for you?"

"I don't want to sound like a complainer, but I wonder if you could talk to the family upstairs for me?" I could tell by the sound of her voice that she was uncomfortable.

"How can help?" I asked.

"Well, it seems that they argue a lot. I know how young people are, but it wakes me up at times and I need my sleep. I work you know?" She continued. "Almost every night, they start arguing. I don't feel quite right asking them to stop. It's kind of embarrassing, you know. Then there's the furniture noise. They throw things around all the time. I can hear the pounding. If you could speak to them about it, I'd appreciate it."

"Mrs. Scott, I'll talk to Ray and Lynn for you. They really are very nice people and I'm sure there will be no problem." I tried to put her mind to rest.

She agreed. "Ray is very nice. He takes the garbage out and shovels the snow. But the noise is a problem. I hate to complain...I really do." She sounded sorry for having to call me, and I could tell she wanted no hard feelings with Ray and Lynn. I assured her it would be handled tactfully.

I didn't quite know what to do. The "arguing" she was hearing was definitely not the other tenants. Ray, being a garbage collector, was up at 4 A.M. on working days. He told me if I needed to talk with him, to call before 9 P.M., for he would be sleeping. I knew that for a fact. Without asking, I knew she must be sleeping in the back bedroom. She was hearing the ghosts echoing on the back porch. I was also sure that the pounding and the furniture being moved was also the ghost, and not the other tenants. I was worried now, because it would only be a matter of time before Mrs. Scott found that the "noise" continued, even when no one was at home.

I felt fortunate that the age difference kept the two families from socializing. If that were not the case, they could have easily put two and two together and knew that the ghosts were doing everything. I wasn't sure of exactly what to do. I knew Mrs. Scott's complaining would continue. It had to, because there was nothing I could do about stopping the arguing, nor the pounding. I felt it was only a matter of time before she would call again. I also felt that it might be that Ray or Lynn might call next, and complain about her arguing. Either way, I was in a dilemma. Again, the Campbell Street building was haunting my thoughts. For a time, I ignored the situation. About two weeks later, Mrs. Scott called again.

"Mr. Becker, you must do something about the noise," she pleaded. "I don't know if you have talked to them or not, but the problem continues.

Their yelling keeps me awake." This time her voice carried the distinct tone of irritation.

"Mrs. *Scott*, I do what I can. It's difficult for me to get involved with their personal problems. Can I ask, in what bedroom do you sleep?" I already knew the answer.

"I sleep in the rear bedroom off of the kitchen." She replied.

"Well, maybe you could sleep in another bedroom, away from the back porch. The sound travels because of the porch." I suggested.

"I'm not moving my bedroom because of them. If I have to, I'll pound on their door the next time it happens. If you can talk to them again, I'd appreciate it." She hung up.

Predictably, the next call I received a few days later, was from *Ray*.

"Ed, I need your help." He demanded. "The woman that rented the first floor is really turning into a bitch. I try to be as nice as possible, but she's always complaining about the noise. I don't think she likes kids. Recently, she started throwing her garbage on the back porch. She used to leave it stacked real nice by the back door, but now, she's just whipping it out. It's a mess." *Ray* was angry.

Stuck in the middle of a situation that was clearly "no win," I tried to placate him. "*Ray*, let me give her a call to find out exactly what her problem is...okay? Why don't you and *Lynn* stop by again at rent time...we can talk?" He agreed.

At that moment, I realized there was only one way out. I had to sell the building. The real estate market had been flat in Chicago for a number of years, so I knew that I would not be in a position of making any money. I had no equity to speak of, and would have to pay real estate commission on the sale. If I could only break even, I would be ecstatic.

I started calling real estate companies. If I signed with a company, I wanted a guarantee that they would advertise and hold an open house. Since real estate commissions were standard, the company that committed to doing the most advertising would likely get my signature on their contract. One by one, the real estate companies visited me and made their sales pitch. All of them sounded alike. Then came *World* Realty.

Ron Benson, the owner of this small real estate company, paid me a visit one Saturday afternoon. Full of enthusiasm, he stated he could easily sell my Campbell Street apartment building. Standing, 6'5", and very thin, he looked the part of a lanky country boy, and had the southern accent to match. The whole time he was trying to convince me that he could sell Campbell Street, he was looking about my apartment.

"Is the apartment above this just as large?" He asked.

"Yes...yes it is. Why?" I asked.

"I have a buyer that is looking for a building like this in this neighborhood. He would pay around $25,000 dollars. Are you interested?"

His comment was almost unbelievable. "$25,000 dollars?" I was astounded, having paid $18,000, just four months ago. I had an instant vision of walking away with $7,000 dollars. This would be enough money to buy a decent house in the suburbs with 20% down.

He continued, and had my full attention. "Sign a contract with me to sell both properties. Sign one for this building for thirty days. I'll not only sell it in thirty days--I'll guarantee that it will be for more than $24,000 dollars, and I'll throw in a color television as a gift...if I do sell it. On the Campbell Street property, sign a contract for 90 days. If I sell it, I'll throw in a gift of a new stereo system."

We shook hands, as it was a deal. He said he would return in a few days with the contracts. After he left, Marsha and I were very excited. Not only had he given us the best deal, *Ron* had more enthusiasm and energy than any sales person I had ever met. If he couldn't sell Campbell Street, no one could.

* * * *

Two days later, the contracts were signed. *Ron* showed me the ad that would appear in both Sunday papers. Good to his word, he was advertising as promised. *Ron* told us to prepare for a lot of activity, as he would schedule showings as quickly as he received the phone calls. With his enthusiasm and his down home manner, it was hard not to believe that the properties wouldn't sell quickly.

That same evening, my tenants were stopping by to deliver their rents. I would have to tell them that we were selling the building. They, too, would have to cooperate, as the prospective buyers would want to look through their building also. This time, *Ray* and *Lynn* were not as happy as with their last visit. Handing me the rent checks, they immediately started talking about the ghost.

"He's playing with the kitchen lights. He turns them on and off. Did you have that problem?" *Lynn* asked.

Marsha and I remained silent, giving the impression that this was most unusual. We did not want to add fuel to their fears.

"Did you ever hear heavy footsteps on the back porch?" She continued.

Again, we remained silent and concerned. I could tell by the expressions on their faces that this was no longer a novelty; it was becoming an aggravation. Marsha and I didn't know exactly what to do. We certainly didn't want to scare them and hurt ourselves by losing our tenants. On the other hand, we knew exactly what they were experiencing and how it would continue to progress. They continued to relate the ghostly activity, while we both tried to appear very surprised. Eventually, they finished their stories and we settled into social conversation. It was then that I laid the bomb shell on them, telling them that we were selling.

I told them I needed their help and wanted them to take responsibility for coordinating the showings at Campbell Street. I would have *Ron* call them directly to schedule the appointments. For this, I would give them one month's free rent after the building was sold, or cash, if they decided to move. *Ray* and *Lynn* agreed to help us. When they left that evening, we felt sad and confused. Marsha and I agreed to encourage them to leave once the building was sold.

* * * *

It was the following Monday when *Ron* called. He said his phone was ringing off the hook with interest in the two buildings. He scheduled a showing of our new building for the next evening. With Campbell Street, he would call our tenants. Because I was asking only $16,500 for the Campbell Street building, which was exactly what I had paid two years prior, it was affordable, and thus, drew plenty of interest. In effect, I was asking less than what I had paid, because of having to pay real estate commission. It was especially true if you took into account all the money and time I had spent on improvements. I could not have cared less; I just wanted it out of my life!

The next night, *Ron* and his buyer showed up at our Ashland Street building. After carefully going over the whole building, they left. We were at a loss to judge the buyer's interest, as the buyer was poker faced as he toured the premises. *Ron* was his enthusiastic self. He was talking a mile a minute, with no loss for words, describing the advantages of purchasing our apartment building. We sat back and hoped for the best.

About two hours after they had left, our doorbell rang. There stood *Ron*, grinning ear to ear, dangling a piece of paper. "Here's your deal." He announced proudly. We invited him in, and he set the contract on the coffee table. It was an offer to buy our new building for $24,500, with a closing date set for sixty days. It was as clean a deal as one could hope for. The buyer had the required 20% down payment, and there were no contingencies. We signed it immediately.

"Well, guess I owe you folks a television. How about a nice 19 inch color table model with remote?" he asked, proudly.

Smiling, we gratefully accepted.

"I had so many calls about the other building, I'll probably sell that one this week also." *Ron* sounded confident. Grabbing the signed contract, he was gone. With the day almost over, I saw no noticeable change in *Ron's* energy level. I could see *Ron* selling three more properties before the night was over. He was a selling dynamo.

Once *Ron* left us, we felt so elated that it was difficult to go to sleep that night. It was unbelievable. *Ron* actually sold our building for a 35% profit, in less than a week. Immediately, we could go shopping in the suburbs for a house. With his display of obvious selling skills, *Ron* left us no doubt that he could sell the Campbell Street property. It would just be a matter of time. We now had no concerns about the building. Our tenants would show it, and *Ron* would sell it. We could just sit back and wait for the contract. The following weekend, we were out shopping for real estate.

It was during our hunt for a new residence that we realized that our experience had left us with a new ability. It was the ability to feel if a house was haunted. It was a bright Sunday morning when we were looking at a beautiful gray stone house. It was in one of the nicer suburbs. Having gone through the real estate listing, everything seemed to meet our needs. It had the location, number of rooms, and school system that we wanted.

The cheery real estate agent drove us for an inspection. As we pulled up to the property, it was all we had imagined from the listing. It was one of the better houses on this block, set within a very nice subdivision. The neighbor's houses looked well kept, and the house itself looked better than the photograph we had seen.

We examined the outside before going in. It was vacant, and the agent unlocked the door for us to enter. I don't think we took ten steps before I stopped dead in my tracks. I looked to my wife, and she, too, appeared concerned. I could feel a presence, distinct and clear, as if I could see it. It was not goose bumps, nor a difference in temperature; it was a pure presence. Marsha felt it too. A quick glance, and we knew we were going no further. I told the agent we were not interested. We turned, and quickly walked out. Back in the car, the agent probed to find out exactly what turned us off. I tried to explain as vague as I could that we didn't like the interior. In a way, it was the truth.

*In the last Forty years, we have encountered a few more haunted houses. We know, because we can feel a presence. It is not always a negative feeling, but it **is** always obvious.*

Eventually, a month later, we purchased a small house in Highland Park, Illinois. It was brown brick three bedroom, with a large yard. Our Campbell Street apartment still hadn't sold. Our dynamic salesman *Ron* was a bit puzzled. He explained that he had showed the building 20 times, with no offers. He said he would keep advertising and showing it until it sold. I had the distinct feeling that this was becoming his personal challenge.

It was not a concern to me as of yet, for our tenants were caring for the building and delivering the rents. They were also coordinating the real estate showings, so there was no reason for me to even visit. We were engrossed with packing and preparing for our move. This time, the preparation was a bit more normal. Marsha was her old self, wanting new curtains and carpeting for the Highland Park house. The month breezed by, and soon it was time to close on the two deals and for us to move.

The weekend before we moved, *Ron* stopped by. He was very confused by his lack of success in selling the Campbell Street building. He still had thirty days left on his contract and for the first time since we met, his enthusiasm was running low. He was very apologetic about the fact that it hadn't sold. He seemed almost embarrassed by his failure. I debated clueing him in on the source of his problem, but decided it best not to. I felt he still had chance at selling it.

We were soon settled into our Highland Park home. Having grown up in the city, suburban living was a dramatic change for me. Marsha was right at home and happy with our new life, but the Campbell Street problems continued. Mrs. *Scott* called and asked to be let out of her lease. She said she couldn't take all the arguing and noise coming from the second floor apartment. According to her, it was non-stop racket, all night long. I had no choice but to let her go. I quickly called *Ray*, asking if he would interview for a new tenant. He said yes, but also that he wanted to stop by and talk with us. It was about a week later that *Lynn* and *Ray* stopped by.

After showing them through our new house, we settled down for some coffee and conversation. As we relaxed in the dining room, I could sense there was something bothering them. I didn't have long to wait before they lowered the boom.

"We're sorry, but we have to move." *Ray* put his head down, staring at his hands that were folded on the dining room table. "It's driving us nuts, living there. It has gotten to the point to where we are scared something bad is going to happen. We went to the Church, but the pastor refused to visit the house for a blessing."

I interrupted. "Father Barnes?" I asked.

"Yeah...yeah that's him. He wouldn't say why. In fact, at first he agreed, until we gave him the address, then it was a fast goodbye. We just can't take it. Could you let us out of the lease early?" he pleaded.

"Sure. I can't keep you there if you're that unhappy. Of course you can leave. We're very sorry you had so much trouble."

As *Ray* and *Lynn* talked about broken dishes and moving brooms, all I could think about was that I had a payment to make and now had no tenants. My salary could cover my house payment with no problem, but I needed the rental income to cover the payment on the Campbell Street building. I was in serious trouble. We ended the discussion by agreeing that as soon as they found a new place, they could move. Once they had left, I immediately dialed *Ron Benson*.

This time it was I that asked *Ron* for a meeting. We agreed to meet at his office in Chicago. I told him that I was desperate to sell the Campbell property. I could lower the asking price by $500 dollars, if that would help. He was not excited, and was confused over his failure at getting an offer.

"In the last three months, I've showed that building a hundred times, with not one offer. I don't understand it. Can I get you to sign up for another 90 days?" He asked.

I felt sorry for him. This lack of success had severely damaged his ego.

"I'm not sure that another 90 days will do it." I replied.

"I know I can sell it. It's just a run of bad luck. All it takes is the right person." It was clear that he wouldn't give up.

At this point, I couldn't keep it a secret any longer. I had to inform him of the problem that his dynamic selling skills could not overcome.

"*Ron*, there is a problem with that building." I began to explain.

"Yeah, it's old and needs a little fix'in up, but the price is right and it should sell." He was committed.

"No...no, I don't mean that. I mean there is something about the building that may be scaring people away." I now had his attention.

"Scaring people?" He looked at me as if I were kidding.

"*Ron*, the place is haunted." When I said the words, I felt that I had made a mistake. *Ron* just stared at me as he sat back in his chair.

"Haunted?" He said it as if he never heard the word in his life.

I continued. "We moved because of ghosts. Now, I can't keep my tenants. My guess is that the people looking at the building are getting bad vibes. They feel the chill or they get goose bumps, and it doesn't feel like home to them. That's why you can't sell it."

He looked totally amazed. "You're kidding me," is all he could say.

"No, I'm not kidding. We tried everything to get rid of them. We had the place blessed, with no luck. We even had it exorcised. The family that owned it has a number of dead family members whose ghosts are there to stay." I let him know that it was hopeless.

"What do the ghosts do?" He asked.

I gave him the capsulated version. "They are very active. They holler, yell, move things, make noise such as footsteps, we've even seen them from time to time. They threw our cat out the second floor window. They have turned off the gas, the electric, and even cry in the night!"

"They threw your cat out the window?" To my surprise, he appeared very interested. "What did they look like? How many times did you see them?" His questions flowed, one after the other, faster than I could answer.

Instead of the expected skepticism, it seemed the *Ron* was excited and interested at the prospect of having a haunted house to sell. We sat for an hour, with me explaining and describing all the ghostly phenomena. *Ron* seemed more enthusiastic about the ghosts than he was about selling the property.

"*Ron*, look, I must get rid of that building. I'll do anything. It looks as though my tenants are moving out...all the tenants. I have a payment to make, and I can't afford to keep it much longer. Even if I find new tenants, I'll be up against the same problem, because eventually they'll move out too. Right now, I have to give their security deposits back, and I'm really screwed." I was looking for ideas, and hoped *Ron* had some.

"This building is really haunted?" He asked again.

"Look *Ron*, I feel uncomfortable saying it, but yes, it is an authentic haunted house. We were on NBC for Christ's sake. Illinois Psychic Research has done studies there. You can call them." I didn't quite know where he was going, but I felt he had a specific interest and maybe an idea. I was floored at his next question.

"How about if I take over the building?" He asked.

"What? You take it? Do you mean, buy it?" I was confused.

"Well, you said you wanted to get rid of it, right?" he asked.

"Yeah," I answered.

"Well, sign it over to me." I was unsure what it meant exactly, not being experienced in real estate.

"What does that mean, 'sign it over.' What about the mortgage?" I asked.

"Well, there's such a thing as a 'quick claim deed.' It is used to immediately transfer properties and responsibilities for real estate. I'll write up the papers, you sign it. I'll take the responsibility for the property and the mortgage. The only problem, is that I don't have the money to buy out your escrow account."

"It's that simple? I don't need an attorney?" I asked.

"Not unless you want one. It's a form that is standard in Illinois. I'll get one and fill it out. We'll sign it and have it notarized. After that, I own the property and am responsible for the mortgage. But, like I said, I don't have the money to repay or buy out your escrow account." *Ron* sounded anxious.

It sounded too good to be true. All I had in escrow reserved for taxes and insurance was about $400 dollars. Not a lot to lose. Of course, I would lose my equity, but that was only about $1000, at most.

"*Ron*, if you really want the building...it's yours. How soon before we can sign the papers?" I asked.

"I can have them on Monday." He replied.

"Are you sure that you want to do this?" I asked.

"Ed, my wife and I have had an interest in ghosts for years. We have attended séances, visited other haunted houses, even traveled at the chance of seeing a ghost or experiencing a ghostly activity. Yes, I'm sure." He was smiling, and excited as a kid at Christmas.

"Call me and let me know what time on Monday. See you." I drove home hoping that he wouldn't change his mind.

Arriving home, I informed Marsha that we were giving the building away...literally. She never raised an eye brow. I explained that we would lose our equity and the money in the escrow account. She wasn't moved and could care less. Marsha's only comment was, "let's wash our hands of it." I could feel the weight coming off of my shoulders. I could only sit back, hold my breath, and hope that *Ron* didn't change his mind. I wasn't home for a half hour when the phone rang. It was our tenant, *Ray*.

"Ed, the real estate man is coming to see us; he says he wants to talk about the apartment. I had the feeling his going to ask some questions about our problem. What should I tell him?" *Ray* knew I didn't want him mentioning the ghosts.

"It's okay *Ray*, tell him. In fact, tell him everything. Don't hold anything back. Get ready for this. He wants the building, but only if it's haunted. So tell him the whole truth. It seems, *Ron* has an interest in ghosts and wants a real haunted house."

"Well, if it's a haunted house he wants, he's going to get one. Maybe we can get the door or the broom to move while he's here." *Ray* sounded ready to give *Ron* a scare.

"Don't hold back. Tell him everything. The more you tell him, the better off I am. It's okay with me."

"Okay, Ed. I just wanted to check with you. See you."

I was surprised. It seemed that *Ron* wanted to be absolutely positive the house was haunted if he was to take on the mortgage. I couldn't believe it. I sincerely hoped that he had no intention of living there and felt strongly that this property was bad luck for anyone that owned it. Days later, *Ron* called to confirm our meeting. He sounded happy about the deal. *Ron* didn't know that I was much happier.

The following Monday, I met him at his office. We signed the papers and his secretary notarized them. It was done. *Ron* was acting like he had just struck gold. He actually presented me with a new stereo system. He said that it was the one that he intended to give me, had he sold the building, per our original contract. He considered it a small payment for keeping the escrow money. He asked if there was anything in the building I wanted. I told him, "No."

I informed him there were tools, furniture, and a few good air conditioners in the basement, along with a few old magazines in the shed. They were all his, as far as I was concerned. I had no desire to revisit the building. I wished *Ron* luck. As we shook hands for the last time, I couldn't help but feel that I had taken advantage of him. I felt that I clearly knew what I had given him, but he had no idea of what he really was given. I knew that *Ron*'s happiness would not last, and I didn't want to be around when it faded. All I could think was, "Tap, tap, no take back!"

We were finally free. As I drove home, I felt more relaxed than I had felt in two years. The Campbell Street building was now history. It was only a bad memory. It would take some time to fully realize that burden we lived with for two years was gone forever. There is no way to describe the feeling of regaining your normal life.

> "I believe with all our modern technology, we don't know much more than we knew 40 years ago. Just imagine if we could establish solid communication with this dimension. Oh, what we could learn."
>
> Edwin F. Becker

Chapter Nine

Epilogue or Aftermath?

Marsha and I were happy to have our lives back. We were glad to know that sounds in the night were from the house settling, and nothing more. We soon realized that we were both hyper-sensitive to any unearthly presence. Many times in the last forty years, we avoided entering various buildings, or exited quickly. We became students of the paranormal, and developed interests in those with unusual abilities. No, I am still not afraid of ghosts, but I respect their presence. I still maintain that humans are far scarier than ghosts can ever be, especially since demons, most always, use a human host.

Although we maintained contact with the psychic Joseph DeLouise, we last spoke over a decade ago. He had continued to communicate his visions, commonly referred to as 'predictions.' He dedicated his life to helping people and using his gifts wherever they were accepted. I don't believe he ever attempted to exorcise a spirit again. A kind and gentle man, I felt a bit sorry for him, for his gift was truly a burden. Just imagine receiving intermittent visions that most always are subject to varying degrees of interpretation. Then facing a public that is all too anxious to criticize and reject.

I re-read Psychic Mission every few years, because so very many predictions have come true. He told of hundreds of thousands of bankruptcies and foreclosures, and two passenger planes colliding over New York City and cascading down in a rain of steel, even before the twin towers were ever built! Just the mention of the prediction of sperm banks in 1970 must have had people howling. I often wonder if author, Tom Valentine, kept any other predictions in his notes that he held back from the book? Tom remains a prolific author.

The Reverend William Derl-Davis, the exorcist, as I learned from Joseph DeLouise, began his own ministry, and soon died a mysterious death at a young age, not too long after the Campbell Street exorcism. I often wonder if this man so dedicated to confronting demons, confronted one that was more than he was capable of defending himself from? I certainly believe in demons, as all one has to do is read the news to find them. However, I will never invite one into my life, nor will I go out seeking them.

Ron, my ghost loving real estate agent, seemed to get more than he bargained for. In trying to locate him only a few years after our transaction, his business was gone. Returning to the Campbell Street property, I found it neglected, and in talking to the locals, I heard he was stricken with a serious illness, was divorced, and had moved away. No one knew who the current owner of the building was. Given this possible streak of bad luck, I imagined that *Ron* had likely made the mistake of taking up residence there, having his life sent into turmoil.

My sister, *April*, has led a life worthy of a book itself. She plowed her way through multiple marriages, substance abuse, has been diagnosed with mental illness, as well as suffered various other illnesses, keeping her from leading anything resembling a normal life. She shuns her children and family, and last she visited me, she slept with the lights and radio on, as this was her habit. She currently lives alone, refusing to see anyone, and even was absent from attending the funeral of our mother. What part the culture of 'mind expansion' played, and/or Campbell Street, can be debated, but the downward spiral began in that apartment.

I never kept track of any of my tenants, but the building seemed to be a curse on many of those that had the misfortune of being involved there. This seemed especially true of anyone that resided within the first floor apartment. In fact, we learned that the late William Derl-Davis made a visit to the first floor apartment after the exorcism, but before his death. I believe the malevolence he felt as *Henry*, he may have decided to confront as a demon. Joseph DeLouise did tell me of Derl-Davis behaving a bit strange before his death.

There is much more a trail of tragedy than I can write about, while still maintaining the privacy of the individuals. I imagine if one had the desire to chronicle the history of the building from 1970 until today, it would make for some very interesting and revealing patterns in all the "owners" lives. Likely, those patterns would show that the family is still very much there and very much in control.

Marsha and I have had many confrontations with ghosts in the past forty years. Most were of no threat, and inexplicably wander the earth. Most seem to do repetitive-type manifestations, whether that is walking the halls, or knocking on walls. We have seen solid ghosts, transparent ghosts, partially visible ghosts, and those that manifest as smoke and as orbs. We have heard them talk, cry, and make various, unintelligible sounds. We once bought an old building in a small Missouri town, and opened a collectable shop. The building held a harmless ghost that we both sensed. I would leave my sound-activated tape recorder there at night, and it would record distinct movement and sounds. Obviously, it regarded us as not being a threat or intrusion. I never had the desire to purchase or use today's sophisticated equipment, for it would only reveal that what we already know--and that is, there is a dimension that we know little about. The total sum of what is known on this subject has not even scratched the surface. Our knowledge and understanding of this whole genre is equivalent to still believing the earth is flat.

For a number of years, we held a strong interest in the paranormal. We met a number of gifted individuals. We also came in contact with a number of ghosts. We learned that there is no pattern or formula to this world of the paranormal. Certain people are given various gifts in unpredictable degrees; whether telekinesis, experiencing visions, or just pure sensitivity. It seems 'we' demand that they use these gifts to do things that they were never intended for, like predict the stock market or Super Bowls. We also demand that they use them at our command. Little is actually known about the fact that our government and YOUR tax dollars have been invested—in the millions—in trying to understand and use these talented people. Yes, our government employs psychics, and has employed them for decades. Marsha and I had the pleasure of spending an evening with the late Olof Jonsson, who, together with NASA, used his ability to mentally communicate with astronaut Edgar Mitchell. This was to be a failsafe method of communication, should all technology fail. This was done over 40 years ago! Without writing a chapter, Olof's display of mind reading and sending messages was beyond amazing.

Without physically being involved, he had Marsha sit in one room reading cards, and I was in another room reciting the thoughts that came spontaneously into my mind. Olof merely acted as a conduit; reading Marsha's mind and sending the information to me. It was the only time in our 45 years of marriage that I read her mind over 50 times without error! Where is Olof when I need him??? God bless him, as he was plagued with naysayers who were always quick to point out his mistakes or failures, as are most gifted individuals.

Having been in the collectable business and owning a store, sent us on numerous house sales. In the process, we encountered many a presence. We encountered a serious spirit that I will only describe as a black, dense, shadow-like presence. We only sensed evil, and no spirit or person associated with it. I found it something to be avoided. Recently, we watched an episode of a ghost hunting series that captured a fleeting glimpse of it on video. As soon as we saw it, we knew what they had captured before they did. We can only sense it is not a ghost, and not to be interacted with in any way. Our senses told us that if demons can travel out of body, this may be what they appear as.

Ghosts are not always scary, mean, or evil. They can be happy or sad, confused or bewildered by their circumstances. At one house sale, we knew as soon as we entered that this was home to a strong entity. As we walked the house, we entered a bedroom where we knew something had occurred. Marsha sensed a strong sadness. As we walked about sensing the vibes, a woman entered and told us of the former owner. She was his daughter, and she told of a father who loved music and was brilliant, and, unfortunately died a slow, painful death in that very room. As she told us of him, I spotted an old Bowler hat, like what they wore during the Roaring 20's. It was like brand new. As soon as I put it on, I felt a surge of happiness. As Marsha watched, I asked to buy it and did, which was typically something we would never do in houses that were *'occupied'*, for fear of bringing along something we did not bargain for. Once outside, she questioned why I broke our rule. I explained that as I put it on, I instantly sensed that this was his *'happy'* hat, and because such, I felt good wearing it. Possibly because he was a musician and loved music, maybe he sensed that in me, but for whatever reason, I only felt happy while wearing my old fashioned Bowler.

I also think I knew what held him earth bound. In his living room was an old, early electronic organ. It was transformed into what looked like an old wired contraption. As I examined it, this man had actually created an electronic organ that would play and record, likely decades before modern technology made it commercially possible. I knew that wherever that contraption went, he would likely follow along.

I would much rather write a novel, than chronicle reality. This was to be a precise record of what transpired for the sake of anyone willing to read it. We know what we experienced. We also know that many other people will likely never forget their encounter at this building. As Carole Simpson reported, *'We, the living, felt a gust of wind that blew the drapes and rattled the Venetian blinds.'* I'm sure she remembers, because I had to provide a bible for her sound tech to sit on, which was the only way he agreed to stay. Without him, there would have been no television recording.

Aside from having a record of what transpired for our family history, I hoped this will serve as a text book for people interested in a true haunting. Spirits are not to be compared to 'Hollywood' movies and fabricated images. Each has its own unique behaviors. Rarely will one confront you and immediately attempt to scare you. In all our experiences, they will initially make you aware of their presence in some subtle manner. Many will ignore you entirely, and their presence may have to be uncovered or investigated for one to become aware. There are spirits that only become active at certain times of the year. There are spirits that only manifest in the daytime or at night. Some can only be heard, while others, only seen. So creating a specific definition of paranormal behavior is impossible.

Our advice to people buying old buildings, is to be aware of your feelings as you examine your potential residence.

Should the rooms seem 'too' cool...take notice.

If the little hairs on your neck rise for no apparent reason...take notice.

If you have a case of obvious goose bumps...be aware.

Should the air feel heavy or thick...pay close attention.

If there seems to be a 'ringing' in your ears...heed the sound.

If you feel immediately agitated for no apparent reason...take notice.

If you feel a breeze and no windows are open...be observant.

Above all, if you feel you are being watched...it's likely you are.

My advice...run--don't walk--and for God's sake, **don't buy it!**

Copy of the sale deed, showing sale of house
for $10. We truly did 'give' it away!